Lucene 4 Cookbook

Over 70 hands-on recipes to quickly and effectively
integrate Lucene into your search application

Edwood Ng

Vineeth Mohan

[PACKT] open source*
PUBLISHING   community experience distilled

BIRMINGHAM - MUMBAI

Lucene 4 Cookbook

First published: June 2015

Production reference: 1220615

Published by Packt Publishing Ltd.
Livery Place
35 Livery Street
Birmingham B3 2PB, UK.

ISBN 978-1-78216-228-5

www.packtpub.com

Credits

Authors

Edwood Ng

Vineeth Mohan

Reviewers

Anders Lybecker

Sujit Pal

Commissioning Editor

James K

Acquisition Editor

Usha Iyer

Content Development Editor

Vaibhav Pawar

Technical Editor

Naveenkumar Jain

Copy Editors

Trishya Hajare

Aditya Nair

Project Coordinator

Kranti Berde

Proofreader

Safis Editing

Indexer

Priya Sane

Graphics

Sheetal Aute

Production Coordinator

Nitesh Thakur

Cover Work

Nitesh Thakur

About the Authors

Edwood Ng is a technologist with over a decade of experience in building scalable solutions from proprietary implementations to client-facing web-based applications. Currently, he's the director of DevOps at Wellframe, leading infrastructure and DevOps operations.

His background in search engine began at Endeca Technologies in 2004, where he was a technical consultant helping numerous clients to architect and implement faceted search solutions. After Endeca, he drew on his knowledge and began designing and building Lucene-based solutions. His first Lucene implementation that went to production was the search engine behind `http://UpDown.com`. From there on, he continued to create search applications using Lucene extensively to deliver robust and scalable systems for his clients. Edwood is a supporter of an open source software. He has also contributed to the plugin `sfI18NGettextPluralPlugin` to the Symphony project.

Vineeth Mohan is a data scientist whose major expertise lies in search analytics and data science. His career started at Yahoo! India, working with a team facilitated by a real-time feed processing platform based on Hadooop across all verticals in Yahoo!. He was also in the team that migrated Right Media technologies to Yahoo! stack. He then moved to Algotree, where he worked across many data science projects such as technical pattern detection in TimeSeries. Later, he designed a real-time news analysis platform based on natural language processing and machine learning approaches. He was also the architect of the search solution for this. Vineeth is passionate about Big Data and data science and has extensive knowledge and experience in Elasticsearch/Solr/Lucene and algorithm design.

About the Reviewers

Sujit Pal currently works in information retrieval and natural language processing in the healthcare industry. He uses a combination of his company's manually curated medical taxonomy and a variety of open-source tools such as Lucene, Hadoop, Mahout, Akka, OpenNLP, and so on, to build the company's semantic search platform. His main areas of interest are search, distributed processing, NLP, and machine learning. He believes in lifelong learning and blogs about his experiences at `http://sujitpal.blogspot.com`.

He works for Healthline Networks, Inc., which is a start-up in the consumer healthcare space.

> It has been a pleasure to review this book. Special thanks to the author and publishing team for making this process so enjoyable.

Anders Lybecker is a technical evangelist for Microsoft and has more than 10 years of experience as a solutions architect, working with multi-billion dollar revenue systems within the travel, finance, and banking industries. A special interest in search technologies and especially Lucene has led to more than a dozen implementations with Lucene, Solr, and ElasticSearch.

Anders has presented at numerous conferences and holds a degree in software engineering, specializing in software development. He blogs about software development including search technologies at `http://www.lybecker.com/blog/`.

www.PacktPub.com

Support files, eBooks, discount offers, and more

For support files and downloads related to your book, please visit www.PacktPub.com.

Did you know that Packt offers eBook versions of every book published, with PDF and ePub files available? You can upgrade to the eBook version at www.PacktPub.com and as a print book customer, you are entitled to a discount on the eBook copy. Get in touch with us at service@packtpub.com for more details.

At www.PacktPub.com, you can also read a collection of free technical articles, sign up for a range of free newsletters and receive exclusive discounts and offers on Packt books and eBooks.

https://www2.packtpub.com/books/subscription/packtlib

Do you need instant solutions to your IT questions? PacktLib is Packt's online digital book library. Here, you can search, access, and read Packt's entire library of books.

Why Subscribe?

- ▶ Fully searchable across every book published by Packt
- ▶ Copy and paste, print, and bookmark content
- ▶ On demand and accessible via a web browser

Free Access for Packt account holders

If you have an account with Packt at www.PacktPub.com, you can use this to access PacktLib today and view 9 entirely free books. Simply use your login credentials for immediate access.

Table of Contents

Preface

Apache Lucene 4 is the backbone of many search engine implementations, including big names such as LinkedIn, Twitter, and IBM. It also serves as a foundation for other open source projects such as Solr and Elasticsearch. We will dive into all the features that Lucene offers and show you easy-to-understand recipes to get you started using Lucene.

What this book covers

Chapter 1, *Introducing Lucene*, introduces you to the core components of Lucene and gives you the know-how to set up Lucene on your own.

Chapter 2, *Analyzing Your Text*, explores a key feature of Lucene called Analyzers. We will show you how text analyzing works and how to customize it to suit your needs.

Chapter 3, *Indexing Your Data*, looks into the data injection process in Lucene and reviews the core concepts, such as norms and similarity.

Chapter 4, *Searching Your Indexes*, will cover the core search components such as FieldCache and TermVectors, and will give you all the knowledge you need to build an effective search engine.

Chapter 5, *Near Real-time Searching*, will show you how near real-time search is achieved via various methods and their trade-offs, so you can make educated decisions when designing your search application.

Chapter 6, *Querying and Filtering Data*, gives you a glimpse of the various querying and filtering features that have been proven to build successful search engines.

Chapter 7, *Flexible Scoring*, takes a technical dive into the mechanics of scoring, how scores are determined, how it affects ranking positions and what you can do to customize it.

Chapter 8, Introducing Elasticsearch, gives an introduction to a Lucene-based open source search solution that gives you everything you need to build a search application in no time.

Chapter 9, Extending Lucene with Modules, explores the additional features, such as spatial search and faceting, that extend Lucene functionalities beyond just text search.

What you need for this book

Lucene is built in Java so all you need is a Java-supported operating system with JDK 1.6 installed. It's preferable to use Oracle JDK; more information can be found here: `http://www.oracle.com/technetwork/java/javase/downloads/index.html`. Lucene's project page can be found at `http://lucene.apache.org/`.

Lucene is a library, so there are no installation steps other than copying the library files. One way to include Lucene into your project is through a Maven repository. Here is a sample Maven dependency description to include in the lucene-core library.

```
<dependency>
    <groupId>org.apache.lucene</groupId>
    <artifactId>lucene-core</artifactId>
    <version>4.10.0</version>
</dependency>
```

Who this book is for

This book is for software developers who are new to Lucene and who want to explore the more advanced topics to build a search engine. Knowledge of Java is necessary to follow the code samples. You will learn core concepts, best practices, and also advanced features, in order to build an effective search application.

Sections

In this book, you will find several headings that appear frequently (Getting ready, How to do it..., How it works..., There's more..., and See also).

To give clear instructions on how to complete a recipe, we use these sections as follows:

Getting ready

This section tells you what to expect in the recipe, and describes how to set up any software or any preliminary settings required for the recipe.

How to do it...

This section contains the steps required to follow the recipe.

How it works...

This section usually consists of a detailed explanation of what happened in the previous section.

There's more...

This section consists of additional information about the recipe in order to make the reader more knowledgeable about the recipe.

See also

This section provides helpful links to other useful information for the recipe.

Conventions

In this book, you will find a number of text styles that distinguish between different kinds of information. Here are some examples of these styles and an explanation of their meaning.

Code words in text, database table names, folder names, filenames, file extensions, pathnames, dummy URLs, user input, and Twitter handles are shown as follows: "we should let Lucene decide which implementation to use by calling `FSDirectory.open` (File path)."

A block of code is set as follows:

```
indexWriter.deleteDocuments(new Term("id", "1"));"));
  indexWriter.close();
```

When we wish to draw your attention to a particular part of a code block, the relevant lines or items are set in bold:

```
Reader reader = new StringReader("Text to be passed");
Analyzer analyzer = new SimpleAnalyzer();
TokenStream tokenStream = analyzer.tokenStream("myField", reader);
```

Any command-line input or output is written as follows:

```
curl -XDELETE 'http://localhost:9200/news/article/1'
```

New terms and **important words** are shown in bold. Words that you see on the screen, for example, in menus or dialog boxes, appear in the text like this: "The **Download** button will take you to all available Apache mirrors where you can download Lucene."

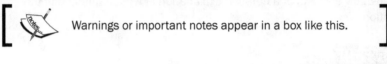

Warnings or important notes appear in a box like this.

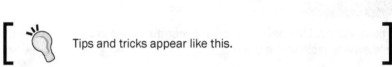

Tips and tricks appear like this.

Reader feedback

Feedback from our readers is always welcome. Let us know what you think about this book—what you liked or disliked. Reader feedback is important for us as it helps us develop titles that you will really get the most out of.

To send us general feedback, simply e-mail feedback@packtpub.com, and mention the book's title in the subject of your message.

If there is a topic that you have expertise in and you are interested in either writing or contributing to a book, see our author guide at www.packtpub.com/authors.

Customer support

Now that you are the proud owner of a Packt book, we have a number of things to help you to get the most from your purchase.

Downloading the example code

You can download the example code files from your account at http://www.packtpub.com for all the Packt Publishing books you have purchased. If you purchased this book elsewhere, you can visit http://www.packtpub.com/support and register to have the files e-mailed directly to you.

Errata

Although we have taken every care to ensure the accuracy of our content, mistakes do happen. If you find a mistake in one of our books—maybe a mistake in the text or the code—we would be grateful if you could report this to us. By doing so, you can save other readers from frustration and help us improve subsequent versions of this book. If you find any errata, please report them by visiting http://www.packtpub.com/submit-errata, selecting your book, clicking on the **Errata Submission Form** link, and entering the details of your errata. Once your errata are verified, your submission will be accepted and the errata will be uploaded to our website or added to any list of existing errata under the Errata section of that title.

To view the previously submitted errata, go to https://www.packtpub.com/books/content/support and enter the name of the book in the search field. The required information will appear under the **Errata** section.

Piracy

Piracy of copyrighted material on the Internet is an ongoing problem across all media. At Packt, we take the protection of our copyright and licenses very seriously. If you come across any illegal copies of our works in any form on the Internet, please provide us with the location address or website name immediately so that we can pursue a remedy.

Please contact us at copyright@packtpub.com with a link to the suspected pirated material.

We appreciate your help in protecting our authors and our ability to bring you valuable content.

Questions

If you have a problem with any aspect of this book, you can contact us at questions@packtpub.com, and we will do our best to address the problem.

1
Introducing Lucene

Many applications in the modern era often require the handling of large datasets. Managing and searching these large collections of information can be very challenging, hence the creation of efficient and high performance search applications has become a necessity. For decades, many data scientists' research focused on information retrieval. One can say that the open source community now bears the fruits of this hard work as many open source data management platforms are developed. The Apache Software Foundation's answer to this: The Apache Lucene has gained popularity recently and is considered the go-to text search framework by many.

Let us take a look at the recipes that we are going to cover in this chapter:

- ▶ Installing Lucene
- ▶ Setting up a simple Java Lucene project
- ▶ Obtaining an IndexWriter
- ▶ Creating an analyzer
- ▶ Creating fields
- ▶ Creating and writing documents to an index
- ▶ Deleting documents
- ▶ Obtaining an IndexSearcher
- ▶ Creating queries with the Lucene QueryParser
- ▶ Performing a search
- ▶ Enumerating results

Getting Lucene and setting up a Lucene Java project serves as a guide for you to get started with Lucene. Instructions to download and set up Lucene are covered in detail in these two recipes. All the recipes that follow introduce basic Lucene functionalities, which do not require in-depth knowledge to understand. We will learn how to create an index and add documents to an index. We will practice deleting documents and searching these documents to locate information. The *Creating fields* section of this chapter introduces you to Lucene's way of handling information. Then, we will learn how to formulate search queries. At the end of this chapter, we will show you how to retrieve search results from Lucene. Hopefully, by completing this chapter, you will gain enough knowledge to set up Lucene and have a good grasp of Lucene's concept of indexing and searching information.

Introduction

Before getting into the intricacies of Lucene, we will show you how a typical search application is created. It will help you better understand the scope of Lucene. The following figure outlines a high level indexing process for a news article search engine. For now, we will focus on the essentials of creating a search engine:

The preceding diagram has a three stage process flow:

- The first stage is data acquisition where the data we intend to make searchable is fetched. The source of this information can be the web, or your private collection of documents in `text`, `pdf`, `xml` and so on.
- The second stage manages the fetched information where the collected data is indexed and stored.
- Finally, we perform a search on the index, and return the results.

Lucene is the platform where we index information and make it searchable. The first stage is independent of Lucene — you will provide the mechanism to fetch the information. Once you have the information, we can use Lucene-provided facilities for indexing so we can add the news articles into the index. To search, we will use Lucene's searcher to provide search functionality against the index. Now, let's have a quick overview of Lucene's way of managing information.

How Lucene works

Continuing our news search application, let's assume we fetched some news bits from a custom source. The following shows the two news items that we are going to add to our index:

```
News Item - 1
"Title": "Europe stocks tumble on political fears , PMI data" ,
"DOP": "30/2/2012 00:00:00",
"Content": "LONDON (MarketWatch)-European stock markets tumbled to
  a three-month low on
Monday, driven by steep losses for banks and resource firms after
  weak purchasing-managers index
readings from China and Europe. At the same time, political
  tensions in France and the Netherlands
fueled fears of further euro-zone turmoil",
"Link" : "http://www.marketwatch.com/story/europe-stocks-off-on-china-
data-french-election-
2012-04-23?siteid=rss&rss=1"


News Item -2
"Title": "Dow Rises, Gains 1.5% on Week" ,
"DOP": "3/3/2012 00:00:00",
"Content": "Solid quarterly results from consumer-oriented stocks
  including Amazon.com
```

```
AMZN +15.75% overshadowed data on slowing economic growth, pushing
    benchmarks to their biggest
weekly advance since mid-March. ",
"Link":
"http://online.wsj.com/article/SB100014240527023048113045773694712
42935722.html?
mod=rss_asia_whats_news"
```

For each news bit, we have a title, publishing date, content, and link, which are the constituents of the typical information in a news article. We will treat each news item as a document and add it to our news data store. The act of adding documents to the data store is called **indexing** and the data store itself is called an index. Once the index is created, you can query it to locate documents by search terms, and this is what's referred to as searching the index.

So, how does Lucene maintain an index, and how's an index being leveraged in terms of search? We can think of a scenario where you look for a certain subject from a book. Let's say you are interested in **Object Oriented Programming** (**OOP**) and learning more about **inheritance**. You then get a book on OOP and start looking for the relevant information about inheritance. You can start from the beginning of the book; start reading until you land on the inheritance topic. If the relevant topic is at the end of the book, it will certainly take a while to reach. As you may notice, this is not a very efficient way to locate information. To locate information quickly in a book, especially a reference book, you can usually rely on the index where you will find the key value pairs of the keyword, and page numbers sorted alphabetically by the keyword. Here, you can look for the word, inheritance, and go to the related pages immediately without scanning through the entire book. This is a more efficient and standard method to quickly locate the relevant information. This is also how Lucene works behind the scene, though with more sophisticated algorithms that make searching efficient and flexible.

Internally, Lucene assigns a unique **document ID** (called **DocId**) to each document when they are added to an index. DocId is used to quickly return details of a document in search results. The following is an example of how Lucene maintains an index. Assuming we start a new index and add three documents as follows:

```
Document id 1:   Lucene
Document id 2:   Lucene and Solr
Document id 3:   Solr extends Lucene
```

Lucene indexes these documents by tokenizing the phrases into keywords and putting them into an inverted index. Lucene's inverted index is a reverse mapping lookup between keyword and DocId. Within the index, keywords are stored in sorted and DocIds are associated with each keyword. Matches in keywords can bring up associated DocIds to return the matching documents. This is a simplistic view of how Lucene maintains an index and how it should give you a basic idea of the schematic of Lucene's architecture.

The following is an example of an inverted index table for our current sample data:

Lucene Inverted Index

and	2
extends	3
Lucene	1,2,3
Solr	2,3

As you notice, the inverted index is designed to optimally answer such queries: get me all documents with the term *xyz*. This data structure allows for a very fast full-text search to locate the relevant documents. For example, a user searches for the term **Solr**. Lucene can quickly locate Solr in the inverted index, because it's sorted, and return DocId 2 and DocId 3 as the result. Then, the search can proceed to quickly retrieve the relevant documents by these DocIds. To a great extent, this architecture contributes to Lucene's speed and efficiency. As you continue to read through this book, you will see Lucene's many techniques to find the relevant information and how you can customize it to suit your needs.

One of the many Lucene features worth noting is text analysis. It's an important feature because it provides extensibility and gives you an opportunity to massage data into a standard format before feeding the data into an index. It's analogous to the transform layer in an **Extract Transform Load** (**ETL**) process. An example of its typical use is the removal of stop words. These are common words (for example, is, and, the, and so on) of little or no value in search. For an even more flexible search application, we can also use this analyzing layer to turn all keywords into lowercase, in order to perform a case-insensitive search. There are many more analyses you can do with this framework; we will show you the best practices and pitfalls to help you make a decision when customizing your search application.

Why is Lucene so popular?

A quick overview of Lucene's features is as follows:

- Index at about 150GB of data per hour on modern hardware
- Efficient RAM utilization (only 1 MB heap)
- Customizable ranking models
- Supports numerous query types
- Restrictive search (routed to specific fields)
- Sorting by fields

▶   Real-time indexing and searching

▶   Faceting, Grouping, Highlighting, and so on

▶   Suggestions

Lucene makes the most out of the modern hardware, as it is very fast and efficient. Indexing 20 GB of textual content typically produces an index size in the range of 4-6 GB. Lucene's speed and low RAM requirement is indicative of its efficiency. Its extensibility in text analysis and search will allow you to virtually customize a search engine in any way you want.

It is becoming more apparent that there are quite a few big companies using Lucene for their search applications. The list of Lucene users is growing at a steady pace. You can take a look at the list of companies and websites that use Lucene on Lucene's wiki page. More and more data giants are using Lucene nowadays: Netflix, Twitter, MySpace, LinkedIn, FedEx, Apple, Ticketmaster, `www.Salesforce.com`, Encyclopedia Britannica CD-ROM/DVD, Eclipse IDE, Mayo Clinic, New Scientist magazine, Atlassian (JIRA), Epiphany, MIT's OpenCourseWare and DSpace, HathiTrust digital library, and Akamai's EdgeComputing platform, all come under this list. This wide range of implementations illustrates that Lucene is a stand-out piece of search technology that's trusted by many.

Lucene's wiki page is available at `http://wiki.apache.org/lucene-java/FrontPage`

Some Lucene implementations

The popularity of Lucene has driven many ports into other languages and environments. **Apache Solr** and Elastic search have revolutionized search technology, and both of them are built on top of Lucene.

The following are the various implementations of Lucene in different languages:

▶   **CLucene**: Lucene implementation in C++ (`http://sourceforge.net/projects/clucene/`)

▶   **Lucene.Net**: Lucene implementation in Microsoft.NET (`http://incubator.apache.org/lucene.net/`)

▶   **Lucene4c**: Lucene implementation in C (`http://incubator.apache.org/lucene4c/`)

▶   **LuceneKit**: Lucene implementation in Objective-C, Cocoa/GNUstep support (`https://github.com/tcurdt/lucenekit`)

▶   **Lupy**: Lucene implementation in Python (RETIRED) (`http://www.divmod.org/projects/lupy`)

- ▸ **NLucene**: This is another Lucene implementation in .NET (out of date) (`http://sourceforge.net/projects/nlucene/`)
- ▸ **Zend Search**: Lucene implementation in the Zend Framework for PHP 5 (`http://framework.zend.com/manual/en/zend.search.html`)
- ▸ **Plucene**: Lucene implementation in Perl (`http://search.cpan.org/search?query=plucene&mode=all`)
- ▸ **KinoSearch**: This is a new Lucene implementation in Perl (`http://www.rectangular.com/kinosearch/`)
- ▸ **PyLucene**: This is GCJ-compiled version of Java Lucene integrated with Python (`http://pylucene.osafoundation.org/`)
- ▸ **MUTIS**: Lucene implementation in Delphi (`http://mutis.sourceforge.net/`)
- ▸ **Ferret**: Lucene implementation in Ruby (`http://ferret.davebalmain.com/trac/`)
- ▸ **Montezuma**: Lucene implementation in Common Lisp (`http://www.cliki.net/Montezuma`)

Installing Lucene

This section will show you what you need, in order to get started with Lucene.

How to do it...

First, let's download Lucene. Apache Lucene can be downloaded from its official download page. As of now, the latest version of Lucene is 4.10. Here is the link to the official page of Lucene: `http://lucene.apache.org/core/`

The **Download** button will take you to all available Apache mirrors where you can download Lucene.

Lucene's index contains `{lucene version}.zip` or `{lucene version}.tar.gz`, including the Lucene core library, HTML documentation, and demo application. Meanwhile, `{lucene version-src}.zip` or `{lucene version-src}.tar.gz` contains the source code for that particular version.

The following is a sample of what the download page looks like:

Index of /apache/lucene/java/4.10.2

Name	Last modified	Size	Description
Parent Directory		-	
changes/	29-Oct-2014 06:27	-	
lucene-4.10.2-src.tgz	29-Oct-2014 06:26	28M	
lucene-4.10.2.tgz	29-Oct-2014 06:26	62M	
lucene-4.10.2.zip	29-Oct-2014 06:26	72M	

How it works...

Lucene is written entirely in Java. The prerequisite for running Lucene is Java Runtime Environment. Lucene runs on Java 6 or higher. If you use Java 7, make sure you install update 1 as well. Once your download is complete, you can extract the contents to a directory and you are good to go. In case you get some errors, the links to the FAQ and mailing list of Lucene users is as follows:

Mailing List:

http://lucene.apache.org/core/discussion.html

FAQ:

http://wiki.apache.org/lucene-java/LuceneFAQ

Setting up a simple Java Lucene project

Having Lucene downloaded, we can get started working with Lucene. Let's take a look at how a Lucene project is set up.

Getting ready

Java Runtime is required. If you have not installed Java yet, visit Oracle's website to download Java. Here is a link to the Java download page: http://www.oracle.com/technetwork/java/javase/downloads/index.html.

You may also want to use an IDE to work on a Lucene project. Many users prefer Eclipse IDE, but you are free to make your own choice, such as NetBeans, or whatever you prefer. If you want to give Eclipse IDE a try, you can refer to the following link: https://www.eclipse.org/downloads/.

Having set up a development environment, let's proceed to create our first Lucene project.

How to do it...

Thanks to the well-organized and efficient architecture of Lucene, the Lucene core JAR is only 2.4 MB in size. The core library provides the basic functionality to start a Lucene project. By adding it to your Java `classpath`, you can begin to build a powerful search engine. We will show you a couple ways to do this in Eclipse.

First, we will set up a normal Java project in Eclipse. Then, we will add Lucene libraries to the project. To do so, follow these steps:

- Click on the **Project** dropdown
- Click on **Properties**
- Select **Java Build Path** in left side of navigation
- Click on the **Libraries** tab
- Click on **Add External JARs...**
- Browse to the folder where lucene-core is located, and then select the core JAR file
- Also, add `lucene-analyzers-common` and `lucene-queryparser`:

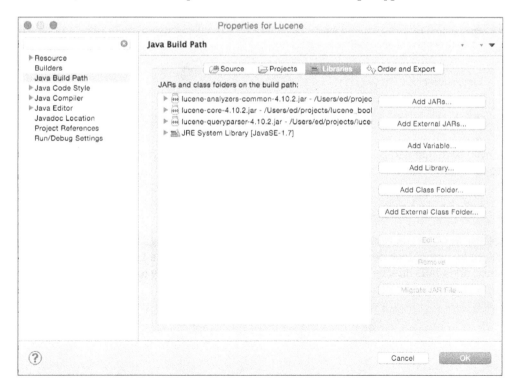

Another way to include the Lucene library is via Apache Maven. Maven is a project management and build tool that provides facilities to manage project development lifecycles. A detailed explanation of Maven is beyond the scope of this book. If you want to know more about Maven, you can check out the following link: `http://maven.apache.org/what-is-maven.html`.

To set up Lucene in Maven, you need to insert its dependency information into your project's `pom.xml`. You can visit a Maven repository (`http://mvnrepository.com/artifact/org.apache.lucene`) where you can find Lucene.

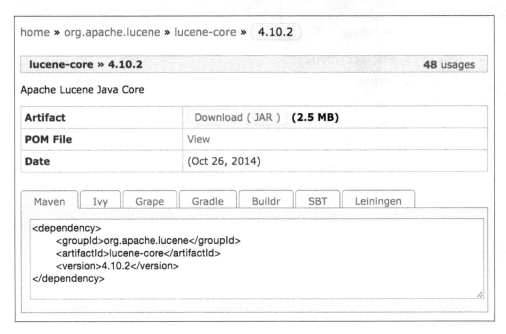

After you have updated `pom.xml`, the Lucene library will show up in your project after your IDE sync up dependencies.

How it works...

Once the JAR files are made available to the `classpath`, you can go ahead and start writing code. Both methods we described here would provide access to the Lucene library. The first method adds JARs directly. With Maven, when you add dependency to `pom.xml`, the JARs will be downloaded automatically.

Obtaining an IndexWriter

The IndexWriter class provides functionality to create and manage index. The class can be found in Lucene-core. It handles basic operations where you can add, delete, and update documents. It also handles more complex use cases that we will cover during the course of this book.

An IndexWriter constructor takes two arguments:

```
IndexWriterDirectoryIndexWriterConfig
https://lucene.apache.org/core/4_10_0/core/org/apache/lucene/index
/IndexWriter.htmlIndexWriter(org.apache.lucene.store.Directory,
org.apache.lucene.index.IndexWriterConfig)IndexWriter
(https://lucene.apache.org/core/4_10_0/core/org/apache/lucene/
store/Directory.html
Directory d, https://lucene.apache.org/core/4_10_0/core/org/apache/
lucene/index/IndexWriterConfig.html"IndexWriterConfig conf)
```

Construct a new `IndexWriter` as per the settings given in the `conf` file.

The first argument is a Directory object. Directory is a location where the Lucene index is stored. The second argument is an `IndexWriterConfig` object where it holds the configuration information. Lucene provides a number of directory implementations. For performance or quick prototyping, we can use **RAMDirectory** to store the index entirely in memory. Otherwise, the index is typically stored in **FSDirectory** on a file system. Lucene has several FSDirectory implementations that have different strengths and weaknesses depending on your hardware and environment. In most cases, we should let Lucene decide which implementation to use by calling `FSDirectory.open` (File path).

How to do it...

We need to first define an analyzer to initialize `IndexWriterConfig`. Then, a Directory should be created to tell Lucene where to store the index. With these two objects defined, we are ready to instantiate an IndexWriter.

The following is a code snippet that shows you how to obtain an IndexWriter:

```
Analyzer analyzer = new WhitespaceAnalyzer();
Directory directory = new RAMDirectory();
IndexWriterConfig config = new
  IndexWriterConfig(Version.LATEST, analyzer);
IndexWriter indexWriter = new IndexWriter(directory, config);
```

How it works...

First, we instantiate a `WhitespaceAnalyzer` to parse input text, and tokenize text into word tokens. Then, we create an in-memory Directory by instantiating `RAMDirectory`. We configure `IndexWriterConfig` with the `WhitespaceAnalyzer` we just created and finally, we pass both Directory and `IndexWriterConfig` to create an IndexWriter. The IndexWriter is now ready to update the index.

An IndexWriter consists of two major components, directory and analyzer. These are necessary so that Lucene knows where to persist indexing information and what treatment to apply to the documents before they are indexed. Analyzer's treatment is especially important because it maintains data consistency. If an index already exists in the specified directory, Lucene will update the existing index. Otherwise, a new index is created.

Creating an analyzer

Analyzer's job is to analyse text. It enforces configured policies (`IndexWriterConfig`) on how index terms are extracted and tokenized from a raw text input. The output from Analyzer is a set of indexable tokens ready to be processed by the indexer. This step is necessary to ensure consistency in both the data store and search functionality. Also, note that Lucene only accepts plain text. Whatever your data type might be—be it XML, HTML, or PDF, you need to parse these documents into text before tossing them over to Lucene.

Imagine you have this piece of text: Lucene is an information retrieval library written in Java. An analyzer will tokenize this text, manipulate the data to conform to a certain data formatting policy (for example, turn to lowercase, remove stop words, and so on), and eventually output as a set of tokens. Token is a basic element in Lucene's indexing process. Let's take a look at the tokens generated by an analyzer for the above text:

```
{Lucene} {is} {an} {Information} {Retrieval} {library} {written} {in}
{Java}
```

Each individual unit enclosed in braces is referred to as a token. In this example, we are leveraging `WhitespaceAnalyzer` to analyze text. This specific analyzer uses whitespace as a delimiter to separate the text into individual words. Note that the separated words are unaltered and stop words (is, an, in) are included. Essentially, every single word is extracted as a token.

Getting ready

The `Lucene-analyzers-common` module contains all the major components we discussed in this section. Most commonly-used analyzers can be found in the `org.apache.lucene.analysis.core` package. For language-specific analysis, you can refer to the `org.apache.lucene.analysis {language code}` packages.

How to do it...

Many analyzers in Lucene-analyzers-common require little or no configuration, so instantiating them is almost effortless. For our current exercise, we will instantiate the `WhitespaceAnalyzer` by simply using `new` object:

```
Analyzer analyzer = new WhitespaceAnalyzer();
```

How it works...

An analyzer is a wrapper of three major components:

- Character filter
- Tokenizer
- Token filter

The analysis phase includes pre- and post-tokenization functions, and this is where the character filter and token filter come into play. The character filter preprocesses text before tokenization to clean up data such as striping out HTML markups, removing user-defined patterns, and converting a special character or specific text. The token filter executes the post tokenization filtering; its operations involve various kinds of manipulations. For instance, stemming, stop word filtering, text normalization, and synonym expansion are all part of token filter. As described earlier, the tokenizer splits up text into tokens. The output of these analysis processes is TokenStream where the indexing process can consume and produce an index.

Lucene provides a number of standard analyzer implementations that should fit most of the search applications. Here are some additional analyzers, which we haven't talked about yet:

- **StopAnalyzer**: This is built with a LowerCaseTokenizer and StopWordFilter. As the names suggest, this analyzer lowercases text, tokenizes non-letter characters and removes stop words.
- **SimpleAnalyzer**: This is built with a LowerCaseTokenizer so that it simply splits text at non-letter characters, and lowercases the tokens.
- **StandardAnalyzer**: This is slightly more complex than SimpleAnalyzer. It consists of StandardTokenizer, StandardFilter, LowerCaseFilter, and StopWordFilter. StandardTokenizer uses a grammar-based tokenization technique that's applicable for most European languages. StandardFilter normalizes tokens extracted with StandardTokenizer. Then, we have the familiar LoweCaseFilter and StopWordFilter.
- **SnowballAnalyzer**: This is the most featured of the bunch. It's made up of StandardTokenizer with StandardFilter, LowerCaseFilter, StopFilter, and SnowballFilter. SnowballFilter stems words, so this analyzer is essentially StandardAnalyzer plus stemming. In simple terms, stemming is a technique to reduce words to their word stem or root form. By reducing words, we can easily find matches of words with the same meaning, but in different forms such as plural and singular forms.

Creating fields

We have learned that indexing information in Lucene requires the creation of document objects. A Lucene document contains one or more field where each one represents a single data point about the document. A field can be a title, description, article ID, and so on. In this section, we will show you the basic structure and how to create a field.

A Lucene field has three attributes:

- ▶ Name
- ▶ Type
- ▶ Value

Name and value are self-explanatory. You can think of a name as a column name in a table, and value as a value in one of the records where record itself is a document. Type determines how the field is treated. You can set `FieldType` to control whether to store value, to index it or even tokenize text. A Lucene field can hold the following:

- ▶ String
- ▶ Reader or preanalyzed TokenStream
- ▶ Binary(byte[])
- ▶ Numeric value

How to do it...

This code snippet shows you how to create a simple `TextField`:

```
Document doc = new Document();
String text = "Lucene is an Information Retrieval library
    written in Java.";
doc.add(new TextField("fieldname", text, Field.Store.YES));
```

How It Works

In this scenario, we create a document object, initialize a text, and add a field by creating a `TextField` object. We also configure the field to store a value so it can be retrieved during a search.

A Lucene document is a collection of field objects. A field is the name of the value pairs, which you may add to the document. A field is created by simply instantiating one of the `Field` classes. Field can be inserted into a document via the add method.

Creating and writing documents to an index

This recipe shows you how to index a document. In fact, here we are putting together all that we learned so far from the previous recipes. Let's see how it is done.

How to do it...

The following code sample shows you an example of adding a simple document to an index:

```
public class LuceneTest {
  public static void main(String[] args) throws IOException {
    Analyzer analyzer = new WhitespaceAnalyzer();
    Directory directory = new RAMDirectory();
    IndexWriterConfig config = new
      IndexWriterConfig(Version.LATEST, analyzer);
    IndexWriter indexWriter = new IndexWriter(directory,
      config);
    Document doc = new Document();
    String text = "Lucene is an Information Retrieval library
      written in Java";
    doc.add(new TextField("fieldname", text, Field.Store.YES));
    indexWriter.addDocument(doc);
    indexWriter.close();
  }
}
```

Downloading the example code

You can download the example code files from your account at http://www.packtpub.com for all the Packt Publishing books you have purchased. If you purchased this book elsewhere, you can visit http://www.packtpub.com/support and register to have the files e-mailed directly to you.

How it works...

Note that the preceding code snippet combined all the sample codes we learned so far. It first initializes an analyzer, directory, `IndexWriterConfig`, and `IndexWriter`. Once the IndexWriter is obtained, a new Document is created with a custom `TextField`. The Document is then added to IndexWriter. Also, note that we call `indexWriter.close()` at the end. calling this method, will commit all changes and close the index.

The `IndexWriter` class exposes an `addDocument(doc)` method that allows you to add documents to an index. `IndexWriter` will write to an index specified by directory.

Deleting documents

We have learned how documents are added to an index. Now, we will see how to delete Documents. Suppose you want to keep your index up to date by deleting documents that are a week old. All of a sudden, the ability to remove documents becomes a very important feature. Let's see how can we do that.

How to do it...

IndexWriter provides the interface to delete documents from an index. It takes either term or query as argument, and will delete all the documents matching these arguments:

- deleteDocuments(Term)
- deleteDocuments(Term... terms)
- deleteDocuments(Query)
- deleteDocuments(Query... queries)
- deleteAll( )

Here is a code snippet on how deleteDocuments is called:

```
indexWriter.deleteDocuments(new Term("id", "1"));"));
indexWriter.close();
```

How it works...

Assuming IndexWriter is already instantiated, this code will trigger IndexWriter to delete all the documents that contain the term id where the value equals 1. Then, we call close to commit changes and close the IndexWriting. Note that this is a match to a Field called id; it's not the same as DocId.

In fact, deletions do not happen at once. They are kept in the memory buffer and later flushed to the directory. The documents are initially marked as deleted on disk so subsequent searches will simply skip the deleted documents; however, to free the memory, you still need to wait. We will see the underlying process in detail in due course.

Obtaining an IndexSearcher

Having reviewed the indexing cycle in Lucene, let's now turn our attention towards search. Keep in mind that indexing is a necessary evil you have to go through to make your text searchable. We take all the pain to customize a search engine now, so we can obtain good search experiences for the users. This will be well worth the effort when users can find information quickly and seamlessly. A well-tuned search engine is the key to every search application.

Consider a simple search scenario where we have an index built already. User is doing research on Lucene and wants to find all Lucene-related documents. Naturally, the term Lucene will be used in a search query. Note that Lucene leverages an inverted index (see the preceding image). Lucene can now locate documents quickly by stepping into the term Lucene in the index, and returning all the related documents by their DocIds. A term in Lucene contains two elements—the value and field in which the term occurs.

How do we specifically perform a search? We create a `Query` object. In simple terms, a query can be thought of as the communication with an index. This action is also referred to as querying an index. We issue a query to an index and get matched documents back.

The `IndexSearcher` class is the gateway to search an index as far as Lucene is concerned. An `IndexSearcher` takes an `IndexReader` object and performs a search via the reader. `IndexReader` talks to the index physically and returns the results. `IndexSearcher` executes a search by accepting a query object. Next, we will learn how to perform a search and create a Query object with a `QueryParser`. For now, let's take a look at how we can obtain an IndexSearcher.

How to do it...

Here is a code snippet that shows you how to obtain an `IndexSearcher`:

```
Directory directory = getDirectory();
IndexReader indexReader = DirectoryReader.open(directory);
IndexSearcher indexSearcher = new IndexSearcher(indexReader);
```

How it works...

The first line assumes we can gain access to a Directory object by calling `getDirectory()`. Then, we obtain an `IndexReader` by calling `DirectoryReader.open(directory)`. The open method in `DirectoryReader` is a static method that opens an index to read, which is analogous to `IndexWriter` opening a directory to write. With an `IndexReader` initialized, we can instantiate an `IndexSearcher` with the reader.

Creating queries with the Lucene QueryParser

Now, we understand that we need to create Query objects to perform a search. We will look at QueryParser and show you how it's done. Lucene supports a powerful query engine that allows for a wide range of query types. You can use search modifier or operator to tell Lucene how matches are done. You can also use fuzzy search and wild card matching.

Internally, Lucene processes Query objects to execute a search. QueryParser is an interpreter that parses a query string into Query objects. It provides the utility to convert textual input into objects. The key method in QueryParser is parse (String). If you want more control over how a search is performed, you can create Query objects directly without using QueryParser, but this would be a much more complicated process. The query string syntax Lucene uses has a few rules. Here is an excerpt from Lucene's Javadoc: `https://lucene.apache.org/core/4_10_0/queryparser/org/apache/lucene/queryparser/classic/QueryParser.html`.

The syntax for query strings is as follows: a Query is a series of clauses. A clause can be prefixed by:

> ▶ A plus (+) or minus (-) sign, indicating that the clause is required or prohibited, respectively.
> ▶ Alternatively, a term followed by a colon, indicating the field to be searched. This enables us to construct queries that search multiple fields.

A clause can be:

> ▶ A term, indicating all the documents that contain this term.
> ▶ Alternatively, a nested query, enclosed in parentheses. Note that this can be used with a+/- prefix to require any of the set of terms.

Thus, in BNF, the query grammar is:

```
Query   ::= ( Clause )*
Clause ::= ["+", "-"] [<TERM> ":"] ( <TERM> | "(" Query ")" )
```

 Note that you need to import `lucene-queryparser` package to use QueryParser. It is not a part of the lucene-core package.

The **Backus Normal Form** (**BNF**) is a notation technique to specify syntax for a language, and is often used in computer science.

How to do it...

Here is a code snippet:

```
QueryParser parser = new QueryParser("Content", analyzer);
Query query = parser.parse("Lucene");
```

How it works...

Assuming an analyzer is already declared and available as a variable, we pass it into QueryParser to initialize the parser. The second parameter is the name of the field where we will perform a search. In this case, we are searching a field called **Content**. Then, we call parse(String) to interpret the search string Lucene into Query object. Note that, at this point, we only return a Query object. We have not actually executed a search yet.

Performing a search

Now that we have a Query object, we are ready to execute a search. We will leverage IndexSearcher from two recipes ago to perform a search.

Note that, by default, Lucene sorts results based on relevance. It has a scoring mechanism assigning a score to every matching document. This score is responsible for the sort order in search results. A score can be affected by the rules defined in the query string (for example, must match, AND operation, and so on). It can also be altered programmatically. We have set aside a chapter to explore the concept of scoring and how we can leverage it to customize a search engine.

How to do it...

Here is what we learned so far and put together into an executable program:

```
public class LuceneTest {
    public static void main(String[] args) throws IOException,
        ParseException {
        Analyzer analyzer = new StandardAnalyzer();
        Directory directory = new RAMDirectory();
        IndexWriterConfig config = new
            IndexWriterConfig(Version.LATEST, analyzer);
        IndexWriter indexWriter = new IndexWriter(directory,
            config);
        Document doc = new Document();
        String text = "Lucene is an Information Retrieval library
            written in Java";
```

```
        doc.add(new TextField("Content", text, Field.Store.YES));
        indexWriter.addDocument(doc);
        indexWriter.close();
        IndexReader indexReader = DirectoryReader.open(directory);
        IndexSearcher indexSearcher = new
        IndexSearcher(indexReader);
        QueryParser parser = new QueryParser( "Content",
        analyzer);
        Query query = parser.parse("Lucene");
        int hitsPerPage = 10;
        TopDocs docs = indexSearcher.search(query, hitsPerPage);
        ScoreDoc[] hits = docs.scoreDocs;
        int end = Math.min(docs.totalHits, hitsPerPage);
        System.out.print("Total Hits: " + docs.totalHits);
        System.out.print("Results: ");
        for (int i = 0; i < end; i++) {
            Document d = indexSearcher.doc(hits[i].doc);
            System.out.println("Content: " + d.get("Content");
        }
    }
}
```

How it works...

The preceding code sets up a StandardAnalyzer to analyze text, uses a `RAMDirectory` for index store, configures IndexWriter to put a piece of content into the index, and uses QueryParser to generate Query object, in order to perform a search. It also has a sample code that shows how to retrieve search results from TopDocs by displaying total hits, and shows matching documents by DocId.

Here is a diagram showing how the search portion works between components:

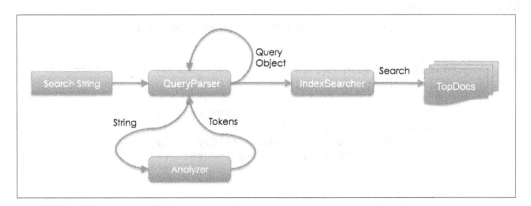

A search string enters into `QueryParser.parse(String)`. QueryParser then uses an analyzer to process the search string to produce a set of tokens. The tokens are then mapped to the Query object, and get sent to IndexSearcher to execute a search. The search result returned by IndexSearcher is a TopDocs object where it contains statistics of total matches and DocIds of the matching documents.

Note that it is preferable to use the same analyzer for both indexing and searching to get the best results.

Enumerating results

We have already previewed how the results are enumerated from the previous sample code. You might have noticed that the major component in search results is TopDocs. Now, we will show you how to leverage this object to paginate results. Lucene does not provide pagination functionality, but we can still build pagination easily using what's available in TopDocs.

How to do it...

Here is a sample implementation on pagination:

```
public List<Document> getPage(int from , int size){
  List<Document> documents = new ArraList<Document>();
  Query query = parser.parse(searchTerm);
  TopDocs hits = searcher.search(query, maxNumberOfResults);
  int end = Math.min(hits.totalHits, size);
  for (int i = from; i < end; i++) {
    int docId = hits.scoreDocs[i].doc;
    //load the document
    Document doc = searcher.doc(docId);
    documents.add(doc);
  }
  return documents;
}
```

How it works...

When we perform search in Lucene, actual results are not preloaded immediately. In TopDocs, we only get back an array of ranked pointers. It's called ranked pointers because they are not actual documents, but a list of references (DocId). By default, results are scored by the scoring mechanism. We will see more about scoring in detail in *Introduction section Chapter 7, Flexible Scoring*. For paging, we can calculate position offset, apply pagination ourselves, and leverage something like what we showed in the sample code to return results by page. Developers at Lucene actually recommend re-executing a search on every page, instead of storing the initial search results (refer to `http://wiki.apache.org/lucene-java/LuceneFAQ#How_do_I_implement_paging.2C_i.e._showing_result_from_1-10.2C_11-20_etc.3F`). The reasoning is that people are usually only interested in top results and they are confident in Lucene's performance.

This code assumes that parser (QueryParser), searcher (IndexSearcher), and `maxNumberOfResults` are already initialized. Note that this sample is for illustrative purpose only and it's not optimized.

2
Analyzing Your Text

In this chapter, we will cover the following recipes:

- ▸ Obtaining a common analyzer
- ▸ Obtaining a TokenStream
- ▸ Obtaining TokenAttribute values
- ▸ Using PositionIncrementAttribute
- ▸ Using PerFieldAnalyzerWrapper
- ▸ Defining custom TokenFilters
- ▸ Defining custom analyzers
- ▸ Defining custom tokenizers
- ▸ Defining custom attributes

Introduction

Before we begin, let's review Lucene's analysis process. We learned about various components in creating and searching an index using IndexWriter and IndexSearcher in the previous chapter. We also looked at analyzer; how it's leveraged in tokenizing and cleansing data; and Lucene's internal index structure, the inverted index for high-performance lookup. We touched on Term and how it's used in querying.

A **term** is a fundamental unit of data in a Lucene index. It associates with a Document and itself has two attributes – `field` (analogous to column name in a table) and `value`. So how does Lucene extract terms from text? You may already be betting on an analyzer. It's correct that an analyzer is responsible for generating these terms. An analyzer is a container of tokenization and filtering processes. Tokenization, as discussed, is a process that breaks up text at word boundaries defined by a specific tokenizer component. After tokenization, filtering kicks in to massage data before outputting to IndexWriter for indexing. This is when tokens are transformed to terms and stored. What the analyzer produces has a significant effect on search, so it's important to understand the analysis process and have the knowledge to choose or build your own analyzer in order to create a good search experience. The following figure illustrates an analyzer facilitating the analysis process:

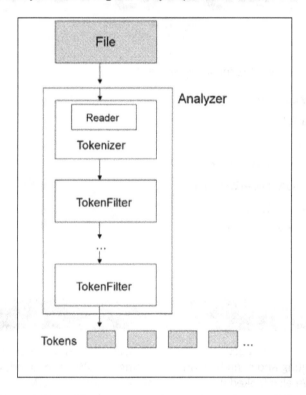

In this illustration, a tokenizer uses a reader object to consume text. It produces a sequential set of tokens that is called **TokenStream**. **TokenFilter** accepts the TokenStream, applies the filtering process, and emits filtered data in TokenStream in return. TokenFilters can be chained together to attain the desired results. A character filter can also be used to preprocess data before tokenization. One example use case for character filters is stripping out HTML tags.

Now we have a fair idea of what an analyzer is. Let's see how this necessary evil can be put to good use:

- **Stopword filtering**: Analyzers can help remove stopwords from text so they are not indexed. Think of words such as a, and, the, on, of, if, and so on. These are words that do not convey any specific meaning. The chance of users searching on these words is very low. Considering the fact that such words usually have high occurrence counts, it is advisable to not index these terms. The process of filtering out such terms from text is called **stopword removal**.

- **Text normalization**: This can be thought of as changing text to conform to a certain standard format, such as lowercasing and the removal of special characters such as the grave accent used in many languages. It is a way to standardize text before it is indexed. This technique helps to improve relevancy in matching search results and also makes comparisons easy and fast.

- **Stemming**: This is another important task that helps to improve accuracy and performance. Stemming in Lucene is a reduction of words to their most basic (root) form, and this process is language-specific. For example, think of the word *run* in the English language. There are different forms of the word depending on how it is used—runs, running, ran, and so on—across documents. From an information retrieval point of view, we are less concerned with these differences.

  Stemming, by itself, is an algorithmic approach that processes terms individually without context, so false positives can be prevalent on words that have similar spelling but very different meanings. However, because the technique can still produce highly relevant results in a majority of searches and can significantly reduce dictionary size by reducing words to root forms, the benefits can outweigh the negatives in some implementations.

  To increase accuracy and reduce false positives, there is a more advanced technique called lemmatization that can be employed to provide stemming that's more context- and language-sensitive. Lemmatization is a linguistic approach to stemming that takes word meanings and potentially grammatical rules into consideration. It will improve matching accuracy but at the cost of computational resources and possibly money because there are currently no lemmatization solutions that are publicly available.

  Lucene provides several stemmer implementations—Snowball, PorterStem, and KStem—that can be leveraged to handle stemmings. The best way to choose the right stemmer is usually the empirical approach as search result quality depends a lot on the types of content being searched on.

- **Synonym Expansion**: Words can be expanded with their synonyms to further improve search quality. As the name suggests, this technique expands a word into additional similar-meaning words for matching, for example, beautiful and pretty or unhappy and sad. Matching synonyms can help bring back more relevant results when searching general ideas.

Obtaining a common analyzer

Lucene provides a set of default analyzers in the `lucene-analyzers-common` package. Let's take a look at them in detail.

Getting ready

The following are five common analyzers Lucene provides in the `lucene-analyzers-common` module:

- `WhitespaceAnalyzer`: Splits text at whitespaces, just as the name indicates. In fact, this is the only thing this analyzer does.

- `SimpleAnalyzer`: Splits text at non-letter characters and lowercases resulting tokens.

- `StopAnalyzer`: Splits text at non-letter characters, lowercases resulting tokens, and removes stopwords. This analyzer is useful for pure text content and is not ideal if the content contains words with special characters such as product model number. This analyzer comes with a default set of stopwords but you can always have the provision to provide your own set of stopwords.

- `StandardAnalyzer`: Splits text using a grammar-based tokenization, normalizes and lowercases tokens, removes stopwords, and discards punctuations. It can be used to extract company names, e-mail addresses, model numbers, and so on. This analyzer is great for general usage.

- `SnowballAnalyzer`: This analyzer is similar to StandardAnalyzer with an additional SnowballFilter for stemming. This provides even more flexibility than StandardAnalyzer. However, SnowballFilter is very aggressive in stemming, so false positive are possible. Lucene is deprecating this analyzer in the upcoming version, 5.0, and recommends you use a language-specific analyzer instead (for example, `org.apache.lucene.analysis.en.*`).

Obtaining the default analyzer is very simple. Note that we don't get to see the actual output, tokenStream, from the analyzer yet. As we progress, we will show you how it's done.

 Make sure the `lucene-analyzers-common.jar` library is also added to the classpath or the corresponding dependency in your `pom.xml`.

How to do it...

Here is how you instantiate an analyzer:

```
Analyzer analyzer = new WhitespaceAnalyzer();
```

You may instantiate any analyzer in the `commons` package in a similar fashion. As you see, it is simple to get default analyzers to work.

How it works...

Let's look at some examples to see how each of these analyzers differs. We will use the following sample text – Lucene is mainly used for information retrieval and you can read more about it at `www.lucene.apache.org`. In the forthcoming sections, we will learn more about customizing analyzers. For now, we shall concern ourselves with output only and review each analyzer's behavior.

First, let's look at `WhitespaceAnalyzer`. As we already learned, a `WhitespaceAnalyzer` splits text at whitespaces. The following would be the output of a `WhitespaceAnalyzer`:

```
[Lucene] [is] [mainly] [used] [for] [information] [retrieval] [and]
[you] [can] [read] [more] [about] [it] [at]
[lucene.apache.org.]
```

Each token is separated in a pair of braces for you to understand clearly. It is quite evident that no normalization has been applied to the text. The split tokens are left as-is. If this analyzer is used exclusively for both indexing and searching, matches will have to be exact (including matching cases) to be found.

Now let's see how `SimpleAnalyzer` analyzes the same piece of text. Here is what we get as output:

```
[lucene] [is] [mainly] [used] [for] [information] [retrieval]
[and] [you] [can] [read] [more] [about] [it] [at] [lucene]
[apache] [org]
```

Tokens are split by non-letters and lowercased in this example. Note the web address is split up because "." is considered as a delimiter. This analyzer expands search capability a little bit by allowing case-insensitive searches (assuming this is used in both indexing and searching, both index and search terms are lowercased prior to processing).

The next one is `StopAnalyzer`:

```
[lucene] [mainly] [used] [information] [retrieval] [you] [can]
[read] [more] [about] [lucene] [apache] [org]
```

This analyzer builds on top of the `SimpleAnalyzer` analyzer's tokenization and filtering with the addition of `StopFilter`. Common English stopwords are removed and tokens are lowercased and normalized, similar to `SimpleAnalyzer`.

Now, let's look at a more sophisticated general purpose built-in analyzer, `StandardAnalyzer`. Here is what it will output:

```
[lucene] [mainly] [used] [information] [retrieval] [you] [can]
[read] [more] [about] [lucene.apache.org]
```

 Note how `StandardAnalyzer` treated the web address `www.lucene.apache.org`.

This analyzer continues to build on top of the features we reviewed so far. It uses a different tokenizer and filter called `StandardTokenizer` and `StandardFilter`, tokenizing text by grammar and removing punctuation. This analyzer is suitable for most implementations as it able to handle special wording such as product model numbers and web addresses (by not breaking them up into separate tokens).

Last but not least, the `SnowballAnalyzer`. Although this analyzer is getting replaced by the language-specific analyzer in `org.apach.lucene.analysis.<language code>` packages, it is powerful nonetheless, because this analyzer handles stemming quite effectively. Here is what the output would be:

```
[lucen] [is] [main] [use] [for] [inform] [retriev] [and] [you]
[can] [read] [more] [about] [it] [at] [lucene.apache.org]
```

Note that several words are changed to their root form (for example, mainly to main), defined by the filter. One of the reasons why this analyzer is getting deprecated is that its performance is not as good as its alternative, another stemmer class based on `PorterStemmer` class. However, some users prefer to use this implementation because the word reduction is more accurate. The new recommended per-language analyzer (for example, `EnglishAnalyzer`) uses `PorterStemmer` (Snowball is also based on Porter) and should give you very good indexing performance and good results that are comparable to `SnowballFilter`.

There's more...

We have seen how various built-in analyzers behave and how each may be suitable for your application. But, in real life, we generally find use cases that differ from the standard offering. In the case of the search application, it is very common that people need to do a lot of customization to make a search engine fulfil business requirements. Luckily, Lucene provide such flexibility where you can create custom analyzers to suit your needs. We will continue to dive deeper and will show you how it's done.

Obtaining a TokenStream

TokenStream is an intermediate data format between components within the analysis process. TokenStream acts as both an input and output format in all filters. For tokenizer, it consumes text from a reader and outputs result as TokenStream. Let's explore TokenStream in detail in this section.

Getting ready

The `Analyzer` class is an abstract base class containing two methods of interest. The first one is `createComponents` (String fieldname, Reader reader). This is where the analyzer is put together by chaining the tokenizer and filters. The second method is `tokenStream` (String fieldname, Reader reader). This is the method we will review in this section. We will use the tokenStream method to return a processed TokenStream so we can examine its content after the analysis process.

How to do it...

We need two arguments to call the `tokenStream` method. The first is a field name and the second is a reader:

```
Reader reader = new StringReader("Text to be passed");
Analyzer analyzer = new SimpleAnalyzer();
TokenStream tokenStream = analyzer.tokenStream("myField", reader);
```

How it works...

An analyzer processes incoming text via a Reader input. Internally, the Reader is passed on to Tokenizer, which turns the text into a TokenStream after it's been processed. From here on, TokenStream is passed around between filters in every step. TokenStream is essentially an enumeration of tokens that you can iterate through. TokenStream extends from `AttributeSource` and it provides an interface to return token attributes and value.

Obtaining TokenAttribute values

With a TokenStream, we can look at how token values are retrieved. From a high level, TokenStream is an enumeration of tokens. To access the values, we will provide TokenStream with one or more attribute objects. Note that there is only one instance that exists per attribute. This is for performance reasons so we are not creating objects in each iteration; instead, the same attribute instances are updated when we increment the token.

Getting ready

There are several types of attributes; each type provides a different aspect, or metadata, of a token. Here is a list of attributes we will review in this section.

This is the token attribute interface description:

- ► `CharTermAttribute`: This exposes a token's actual textual value, equivalent to a term's value.

- ► `PositionIncrementAttribute`: This returns the position of the current token relative to the previous token. This attribute is useful in phrase-matching as the keyword order and their positions are important. If there are no gaps between the current token and the previous token (for example, no stop words in between), it will be set to its default value, 1.

- ► `OffsetAttribute`: This gives you information about the start and end positions of the corresponding term in the source text.

- ► `TypeAttribute`: This is available if it is used in the implementation. This is usually used to identify the data type.

- ► `FlagsAttribute`: This is somewhat similar to `TypeAttribute`, but it serves a different purpose. Suppose you need to add specific information about a token and that information should be available down the analyzer chain, you can pass it as flags. TokenFilters can perform any specific action based on the flags of the token.

- ► `PayloadAttribute`: This stores the payload at each index position and is generally useful in scoring when used with Payload-based queries. Because it's stored at each position, it is best to have a minimum number of bytes per term in the index to minimize overloading the index with a massive amount of data.

How to do it...

Now we will see Attribute retrieval in action. In this sample, we will use `StandardAnalyzer` to process the input text and `OffsetAttribute` and `CharTermAttribute` to return each token's value and its offsets. Here is the sample code:

```
StringReader reader = new StringReader("Lucene is mainly used for
information retrieval and you can read more about it at lucene.apache.
org.");
StandardAnalyzer wa = new StandardAnalyzer();
TokenStream ts = null;

try {
    ts = wa.tokenStream("field", reader);
```

```
    OffsetAttribute offsetAtt = ts.addAttribute(OffsetAttribute.
class);
    CharTermAttribute termAtt = ts.addAttribute(CharTermAttribute.
class);

    ts.reset();

    while (ts.incrementToken()) {
        String token = termAtt.toString();
        System.out.println("[" + token + "]");
        System.out.println("Token starting offset: " + offsetAtt.
startOffset());
        System.out.println(" Token ending offset: " + offsetAtt.
endOffset());
        System.out.println("");
    }

    ts.end();
} catch (IOException e) {
    e.printStackTrace();
} finally {
    ts.close();
    wa.close();
}
```

 Keep in mind that Attribute objects are reused in each iteration as we increment tokens for performance and efficient memory management.

How it works...

In this sample, we are breaking down this text – Lucene is mainly used for information retrieval and you can read more about it at www.lucene.apache.org. using StandardAnalyzer. Note that we put a try catch block around TokenStream retrieval and its iteration. This is so we can handle IOException and use the finally block to cleanly close the TokenStream and Analyzer. The following is a step-by-step guide on what's happening in the sample code:

1. To start processing text, we turn our input stream into StringReader to pass into the Analyzer's tokenStream method.

2. Then we instantiate two attribute objects, OffsetAttribute and CharTermAttribute.

3. The attribute objects are then registered in TokenStream by calling its `addAttribute` method.

4. Note that we call `ts.reset()` to reset TokenStream to the beginning. This call is necessary prior to every iteration routine to ensure we always iterate from the beginning.

5. We iterate TokenStream in a `while` loop by calling `ts.incrementToken()`. The loop exits when `incrementToken()` returns false.

6. We call `termAtt.toString()` to return the current token's value and call the `startOffset()` and `endOffset()` methods of `offsetAtt` to get the offset. Note that the variables `termAtt` and `offsetAtt` are reused in every iteration.

7. Now we call `ts.end()` to end the TokenStream. This call signals the current TokenStream handler to execute any end-of-stream operations.

8. And lastly, we call the `close()` method to close out the TokenStream and Analyzer to release any resources used during the analysis process.

Using PositionIncrementAttribute

The `PositionIncrementAttribute` class shows the position of the current token relative to the previous token. The default value is 1. Any value greater than 1 implies that the previous token and the current token are not consecutive – there is a gap between the two tokens where some tokens (for example, stopwords) are omitted. This attribute is useful in phrase matching, where the position and order of words matters. For example, say you want to execute an exact phrase match. As we step through TokenStream, the `PositionIncrementAttribute` class on each matching token should be *1* so we know the phrase we are matching is matched word for word exactly in the same order as the search phrase.

Another use of this attribute is synonym matching in a phrase query. Synonyms can be inserted into the TokenStream following the term that's being expanded. The position increments for the synonyms would set to 0 as that indicates the synonym term is at the same position as the source term (the previous token). That way, the phrase *Lucene is great for search* would match *Lucene is excellent for search* (assuming *great* is synonymous with *excellent* in the chosen synonym filter).

Getting ready

`PositionIncrementAttribute` can be retrieved by calling `addAttribute(PositionIncrementAttribute.class)` on the TokenStream object. As we already learned, the attribute is updated when we call `incrementToken` to iterate through the tokens. To illustrate how this attribute is used, we are going to write a simple Filter that will skip stopwords and set increment positions accordingly.

How to do it...

Here is a sample code snippet:

```
public class MyStopWordFilter extends TokenFilter {

    private CharTermAttribute charTermAtt;
    private PositionIncrementAttribute posIncrAtt;

    public MyStopWordFilter(TokenStream input) {
      super(input);
      charTermAtt = addAttribute(CharTermAttribute.class);
      posIncrAtt = addAttribute(PositionIncrementAttribute.class);
    }

    @Override
    public boolean incrementToken() throws IOException {

      int extraIncrement = 0;
      boolean returnValue = false;
      while (input.incrementToken()) {
        if (StopAnalyzer.ENGLISH_STOP_WORDS_SET.contains
          (charTermAtt.toString())) {
            extraIncrement++;// filter this word
            continue;
          }

        returnValue = true;

        break;
      }

      if(extraIncrement>0){
        posIncrAtt.setPositionIncrement
          (posIncrAtt.getPositionIncrement()+extraIncrement);
      }
      return returnValue;
    }
}
```

How it works...

In this example, we obtain two attributes, `CharTermAttribute` (for text value retrieval) and `PositionIncrementAttribute` (to set the position increment value). Then we call `input.incrementToken()` to iterate through the TokenStream (input is a variable in TokenFilter that points to the incoming TokenStream). In each iteration, we check if the current token is a stopword. If it's a stopword, we increment `extraIncrement` by 1 to account for the filtered stopword. The while loop exits either if we find a non-stopword or if we exhaust the list of tokens. An `PositionIncrementAttribute` class is set on the next non-stopword token with the addition of `extraIncrement`. The updated increment tells you how many tokens this filter filters out.

Using PerFieldAnalyzerWrapper

Imagine you are building a search engine for a retailer website where you need to index fields such as product title, description, sku, category, rating, reviews, and so on. Using a general-purpose analyzer for all these fields may not be the best approach. It would work to some degree but you will soon learn that there are cases where a general-purpose analyzer may return undesired results.

For example, say you have a sku "AB-978" and are using StandardAnalyzer for all fields. The analyzer would break up "AB-978" into two, [ab] [978]. This will have an adverse effect in search accuracy because differences in sku between closely related products may vary very little. We may have another product with sku "AB-978-1". In StandardAnalyzer, both strings would produce these two tokens [ab] [978]. When a user searches for the term "AB-978", both products would be treated with equal weight in the search results. So, there is a possibility that product "AB-978-1" may rank higher than "AB-978" in the search results.

You may be wondering if it's possible to use different analysis processes between fields so we can apply one method on one field and apply another one for a different field. The answer is yes and Lucene provides a per-field analyzer wrapper class to let us achieve that. The `PerFieldAnalyzerWrapper` constructor accepts two arguments, a default analyzer and a Map of field to analyzer mapping. During the analysis process, if a field is found in the Map, the associated Analyzer will be used. Otherwise, the process will use the default analyzer.

Getting ready

Let's go through an example to demonstrate how `PerFieldAnalyzerWrapper` works. In our scenario, we will attempt to analyze text on a known field mapped in `PerFieldAnalyzerWrapper` and analyze the same text on an unmapped field. We will see how the output differs in this exercise.

How to do it...

Here is the code snippet:

```
Map<String,Analyzer> analyzerPerField = new
  HashMap<String,Analyzer>();
analyzerPerField.put("myfield", new WhitespaceAnalyzer());
PerFieldAnalyzerWrapper defanalyzer = new
  PerFieldAnalyzerWrapper(new StandardAnalyzer(),
    analyzerPerField);
TokenStream ts = null;
OffsetAttribute offsetAtt = null;
CharTermAttribute charAtt = null;
try {
  ts = defanalyzer.tokenStream("myfield", new
    StringReader("lucene.apache.org AB-978"));
  offsetAtt = ts.addAttribute(OffsetAttribute.class);
  charAtt = ts.addAttribute(CharTermAttribute.class);
  ts.reset();
  System.out.println("== Processing field 'myfield' using
    WhitespaceAnalyzer (per field) ==");
  while (ts.incrementToken()) {
    System.out.println(charAtt.toString());
    System.out.println("token start offset: " +
      offsetAtt.startOffset());
    System.out.println("  token end offset: " +
      offsetAtt.endOffset());
  }
  ts.end();

  ts = defanalyzer.tokenStream("content", new
    StringReader("lucene.apache.org AB-978"));
  offsetAtt = ts.addAttribute(OffsetAttribute.class);
  charAtt = ts.addAttribute(CharTermAttribute.class);
  ts.reset();
  System.out.println("== Processing field 'content' using
    StandardAnalyzer ==");
  while (ts.incrementToken()) {
    System.out.println(charAtt.toString());
    System.out.println("token start offset: " +
      offsetAtt.startOffset());
```

```
        System.out.println(" token end offset: " +
          offsetAtt.endOffset());
      }
      ts.end();
    }
    catch (IOException e) {
      e.printStackTrace();
    }
    finally {
      ts.close();
    }
```

How it works...

First, we initialize a `PerFieldAnalyzerWrapper` class with a single field mapping
for `myfield` that maps to a `WhitespaceAnalyzer`. The default analyzer is set to
`StandardAnalyzer`. Then we go through the usual steps in setting attribute objects for
acquiring attributes for `OffsetAttribute` and `CharTermAttribute`. We run through the
same routine twice, once where we process text in the matching field `myfield` and a second
time where we process text in the non-matching field `content`. Note that the input string
(lucene.apache.org AB-978) for both routines is identical.

When you execute this code, the first routine will output two tokens, [lucene.apache.org] and
[AB-978], because `WhitespaceAnalyzer` was applied. The `PerFieldAnalyzerWrapper`
class found a match in its mapping for the field `myfield`. In the second routine, three tokens
will output instead, [lucene.apache.org] [ab] [978]. The field content was not found, so the
default analyzer `StandardAnalyzer` was applied.

Defining custom TokenFilters

Sometimes, search behaviors may be so specific that we need to create a custom TokenFilter
to achieve those behaviors. To create a custom filter, we will extend from the TokenFilter class
and override the `incrementToken()` method.

We will create a simple word-expanding TokenFilter that expands courtesy titles from the short
form to the full word. For example, *Dr* expands to *doctor*.

How to do it...

Here is the sample code:

```
public class CourtesyTitleFilter extends TokenFilter {
    Map<String,String> courtesyTitleMap = new
HashMap<String,String>();
```

```
        private CharTermAttribute termAttr;
        public CourtesyTitleFilter(TokenStream input) {
            super(input);
            termAttr = addAttribute(CharTermAttribute.class);
            courtesyTitleMap.put("Dr", "doctor");
            courtesyTitleMap.put("Mr", "mister");
            courtesyTitleMap.put("Mrs", "miss");
        }
        public boolean incrementToken() throws IOException {
            if (!input.incrementToken())
                return false;
            String small = termAttr.toString();
            if(courtesyTitleMap.containsKey(small)) {
                termAttr.setEmpty().append(courtesyTitleMap.get(small));
            }
            return true;
        }
    }
```

How it works...

We create the `CourtesyTitleFilter` class by extending TokenFilter. In its constructor, we initialize a `CharTermAttribute` instance for reading the token value and initialize `courtesyTitleMap` with the short form and word mapping for our conversion. In the overridden method, `incrementToken()`, we first check if the input (inputting TokenStream) still has a token. If no token is found, it exits with a false value. Then it checks if the token exists in `courtesyTitleMap`. If a mapping is found, it resets the token value with `CharTermAttribute`, setting the attribute `empty` by calling `setEmpty()` and appending it with the new value from `courtesyTitleMap`.

When you run this code as part of an analysis process that splits text by whitespaces and applies a lowercase filter at the end, the string `Dr Watson` would become `[doctor]` `[watson]` in output.

Defining custom analyzers

It's necessary to create a custom analyzer when the built-in analyzers do not provide the needed behaviors for your search application. To continue with our CourtesyTitleFilter example, we will create `CourtesyTitleAnalyzer`.

The anatomy of an analyzer includes one tokenizer and one or more TokenFilters. We will build an Analyzer by extending from the `Analyzer` abstract class and implement the createComponents method.

How to do it...

Here is the sample code for `CourtesyTitleAnalyzer`:

```
public class CourtesyTitleAnalyzer extends Analyzer {

    @Override
    protected TokenStreamComponents createComponents(String
        fieldName, Reader reader) {
    Tokenizer letterTokenizer = new LetterTokenizer(reader);
    TokenStream filter = new CourtesyTitleFilter
        (letterTokenizer);
    return new TokenStreamComponents(letterTokenizer,
        filter);
    }
}
```

How it works...

An Analyzer is created by extending from the `Analyzer` abstract class as shown in this example. Then we override the `createComponents` method, adding a `LetterTokenizer` to split text by non-letter characters and `CourtesyTitleFilter` as a TokenFilter. Finally, we return a new `TokenStreamComponents` instance initialized by the instantiated `Tokenizer` and `TokenFilter`.

Note that the only method we need to override is `createComponents`. We don't need to override the constructor to build our Analyzer because components are not added during construction; they are added when the `createComponents` method is called. Therefore, we override the `createComponents` method to customize an Analyzer. Also note that we cannot override the `tokenStream` method because it's declared as final.

Defining custom tokenizers

Although there are several excellent built-in tokenizers in Lucene, you may still find yourself needing something to behave slightly differently. You will then have to custom-build a Tokenizer. Lucene provides a character-based tokenizer called `CharTokenizer` that should be suitable for most types of tokenizations. You can override its `isTokenChar` method to determine what characters should be considered as part of a token and what characters should be considered as delimiters. It's worthwhile to note that both `LetterTokenizer` and `WhitespaceTokenizer` extend from `CharTokenizer`.

How to do it...

In this example, we will create our own tokenizer that splits text by space only. It is similar to `WhitespaceTokenizer` but this one is simpler. Here is the sample code:

```
public class MyTokenizer extends CharTokenizer {

    public MyTokenizer(Reader input) {
        super(input);
    }

    public MyTokenizer(AttributeFactory factory, Reader input) {
        super(factory, input);
    }

    @Override
    protected boolean isTokenChar(int c) {
        return !Character.isSpaceChar(c);
    }
}
```

How it works...

In this example, we extend from an abstract class called `CharTokenizer`. As described earlier, this is a character-based tokenizer. To use `CharTokenizer`, you need to override the `isTokenChar` method. In this method, you get to examine the input stream (via Reader) character by character and determine whether to treat the character as a token character or a delimiting character. It handles the complexity of token extraction from a Reader for you so you can focus on the business logic of how text should be tokenized. We want to build a tokenizer that splits text by space only, so we leverage the `isSpaceChar` method from the `character` class to determine if the character is a space. If it's a space, it returns false, which means it's a token character. Otherwise, the character will be treated as a delimiting character and a new token will form afterwards.

Defining custom attributes

The built-in `Attribute` classes should suffice for most of the implementation, but if you encounter a situation where you need a custom attribute, you may do so by creating your own `Attribute` class. In this section, we will create an `Attribute` interface and then an implementation class extending `AttributeImpl` and a `TokenFilter` that will set the attribute value. Our example will be a simple exercise where we determine the gender for a token based on specific words. This is purely for illustration purpose only, so this is by no means a useful implementation for any application.

How to do it...

First, let's start with an interface:

```
public interface GenderAttribute extends Attribute {

    public static enum Gender {Male, Female, Undefined};

    public void setGender(Gender gender);

    public Gender getGender();
}
```

Let's now apply an implementation class extending from `AttributeImpl`:

```
public class GenderAttributeImpl extends AttributeImpl implements
  GenderAttribute {

    private Gender gender = Gender.Undefined;

    public void setGender(Gender gender) {
      this.gender = gender;
    }

    public Gender getGender() {
      return gender;
    };
    @Override
    public void clear() {
        gender = Gender.Undefined;
    }

    @Override
    public void copyTo(AttributeImpl target) {
        ((GenderAttribute) target).setGender(gender);
    }
}
```

Finally, we create a TokenFilter to let us set the Attribute value:

```
public class GenderFilter extends TokenFilter {
    GenderAttribute genderAtt = addAttribute(GenderAttribute.class);
    CharTermAttribute charTermAtt = addAttribute(CharTermAttribute.
class);

    protected GenderFilter(TokenStream input) {
        super(input);
    }

    public boolean incrementToken() throws IOException {
        if (!input.incrementToken()) { return false; }
        genderAtt.setGender(determineGender(charTermAtt.toString()));
        return true;
    }

    protected GenderAttribute.Gender determineGender(String term) {
        if (term.equalsIgnoreCase("mr") || term.
equalsIgnoreCase("mister")) {
            return GenderAttribute.Gender.Male;
        } else if (term.equalsIgnoreCase("mrs") || term.
equalsIgnoreCase("misters")) {
            return GenderAttribute.Gender.Female;
        }
        return GenderAttribute.Gender.Undefined;
    }
}
```

How it works...

Part of the requirement of creating a custom `Attribute` class is the creation of an interface that's based on attribute and an implementation that's based on `AttributeImpl`. The names of the classes are important because Lucene looks for the `Impl` suffix to locate the implementation class of an `Attribute` interface.

Let's dive into the details of the implementation now. In `GenderAttribute`, we defined it as an interface-extending attribute. This is what will be passed into the `addAttribute` method to register this attribute to a TokenStream. We defined an `enum` that holds three values – Male, Female, and Undefined. We also defined a setter and a getter for the gender variable.

In the implementation class `GenderAttributeImpl`, we have a private variable, `gender`, that will store the gender value for a token and we have implementations for the setter and getter defined in the interface. We also overrode two methods – `clear` and `copyTo`. Overriding the `clear` method allows us to customize how we clear the attribute value and overriding `copyTo` allows us to customize how copy attribute is done.

And lastly, we have `GenderFilter`, which extends `TokenFilter`. We instantiate two attributes – `GenderAttribute` (what we defined) and `CharTermAttribute`. We will use `CharTermAttribute` to return the textual value of a token so we can determine the gender from it. We implemented `incrementToken` so we can insert the gender into `GenderAttribute` when `incrementToken` is called. The gender is determined in the `determineGender` method. The implementation of this method just simply checks if the current term matches a certain courtesy title to determine the gender. Then it returns the gender value. This implementation is intentionally simplified, as the robustness of this method is not the priority of this section.

3
Indexing Your Data

We will cover the following topics in this chapter:

- ▸ Obtaining an IndexWriter
- ▸ Creating a StringField
- ▸ Creating a TextField
- ▸ Creating a numeric field
- ▸ Creating a DocValue field
- ▸ Transactional commits and index versioning
- ▸ Reusing field and document objects per thread
- ▸ Delving into field norms
- ▸ Changing similarity implementation used during indexing

Introduction

An index in a search engine can make or break an application. A well-tuned index with a well-thought out indexing process will not only reduce future maintenance cost, but will also reduce any potentially expensive application failures due to corruption in the data and/or a break down in the data processing pipeline. We will dive into the indexing process more in this chapter to equip you with the knowledge you need to build a stable search application.

So far, we covered the basics of setting up Lucene, injecting data, and configuring the analysis process. In this chapter, we will explore the indexing process to learn more about the advanced techniques in configuring and tuning the process.

Let's review what we've learned already on Lucene's internal index structure so far, regarding the inverted index. Consider the following sentences passing through `StandardAnalyzer` before being added to our index:

```
Humpty Dumpty sat on a wall,
Humpty Dumpty had a great fall.
All the king's horses and all the king's men
Couldn't put Humpty together again
```

We will treat each sentence as a document. Below is a figure showing what the documents and inverted index look like:

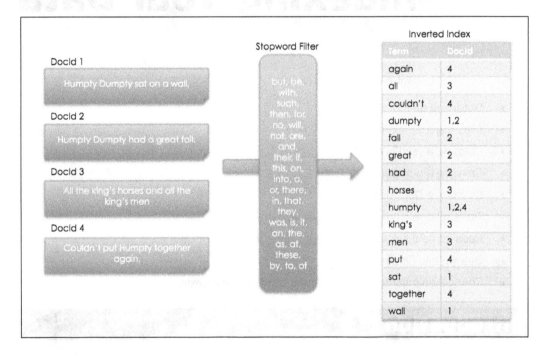

The preceding diagram illustrates that the Analyzer filters out stopwords and the resulting tokens, generated by the tokenization process, are extracted and stored as individual terms. Note that the inverted index contains a sorted list of terms with an associated DocId for each term. The term to DocId relationship is a one-to-many relationship. The analysis process and the inverted index are important concepts for understanding how to use Lucene effectively.

 The diagram does not represent the exact process workflow in Lucene; it is mainly for illustration purpose only.

Another important concept to learn is the segmented nature of Lucene's index file format. Index files are physically separated by segments and they follow a naming standard, where files are named `segments_1`, then `segments_2`, and so on. All files belonging to the same segment share the same filename with varying extensions. Each segment is a fully independent index that can be searched separately. Simply adding new documents can generate a new segment.

Here is an illustration of index segments:

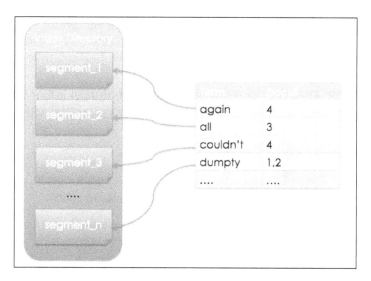

The terms and documents can exist in any of the segments, depending on when the new documents and terms are added. The `IndexReader` attributes will merge the index segments internally so that you can access a coherent index without having to consider the index segmentation.

Obtaining an IndexWriter

We have seen how an IndexWriter is obtained just by simply initialized with an Analyzer and `IndexWriterConfig`. The default initialization behavior usually works well for the majority of the time. However, there may be situations where you need finer control during the initialization sequence. For example, when the default behavior creates a new index if an existing index doesn't exist already. This may not be ideal in a production environment where an index should always exist. Generating a new index will automatically hide the issue that an index is missing. Perhaps there was a glitch in the backup routine where it accidentally removed the index, or there was a data corruption issue that somehow wiped out the index directory. In any case, it would be beneficial if we are aware of the indexing status and alerted when issues are detected.

Lucene does provide options to control how an index is opened. We will talk about each option in detail in this section and show you how it is done.

The `IndexWriterConfig`, a configuration object where you set the `IndexWriter` attributes, provides three `OpenMode` options to open an index. The options are:

- **APPEND**: This opens an existing index on a directory and allows `IndexWriter` to update an index. No new index will be created with this option. If an existing index doesn't exist already, an exception `IndexNotFoundException` will be thrown.

- **CREATE**: This creates a new index, if a directory does not contain one already, or it replaces an existing index. This option will always create a fresh index on the supplied directory. Be careful when using this option because it will overwrite an existing index when one already exists.

- **CREATE_OR_APPEND**: This is the default option. If no index is found in the supplied directory, a new index is created. Otherwise, `IndexWriter` will append to the existing index. This is a safe option.

How to do it...

Here is a sample code snippet showing how to set the `OpenMode` option:

```
FSDirectory directory = FSDirectory.open(new File(indexPath));
Analyzer analyzer = new StandardAnalyzer();
IndexWriterConfig config = new
   IndexWriterConfig(Version.LATEST, analyzer);
config.setOpenMode(IndexWriterConfig.OpenMode.CREATE);
config.setRAMBufferSizeMB(64);
config.setMaxBufferedDocs(4000);
IndexWriter indexWriter = new IndexWriter(directory, config);
```

How it works...

In this code snippet, we first initialize a directory object with an `indexPath` (assuming it is already defined, pointing at an index directory) and set up an `Analyzer` and `IndexWriterConfig`. Then, we set the `OpenMode` on `IndexWriterConfig` before we pass it onto an `IndexWriter`. The `setOpenMode` method is where you can set the desired `OpenMode`.

In addition to `OpenMode`, `IndexWriterConfig` has many other tuneable options. A notable option is `setRAMBufferSizeMB(double)`. This option allows you to tune the amount of RAM to use for buffering changes before being flushed to the directory. The buffer is default to 16 MB. In our example, we set it to 64 MB. Another useful tuning option is `setMaxBufferedDocs(int)`; it lets you set the minimum number of documents required before the buffered documents are flushed as a new segment. The default value is *1000*, but we set it to *4000* in our sample code. When both options are set, the buffer is flushed when whichever condition comes first.

 Note that the changes to index are not visible until `commit()` or `close()` is called on `IndexWriter`.

Creating a StringField

Let's look at a quick recap of field objects in Lucene; they are part of a document containing information about the document. A field is composed of three parts: name, type, and value. Values can be text, binary, or numeric. A field can also be stored in the index so that their values are returned along with hits. Lucene provides a number of field implementations out of the box that are suitable for most applications. In this section, we will cover a field implementation that stores the literal string, `StringField`. Any value stored in this field can be indexed, but not tokenized. The entire string is treated as a single token.

So why don't we want to tokenize the text since we have talked about tokenization for quite a bit already? Consider that a part of a document is an address and that you have fields such as street address, city, state, and country contained within it. It's not a very good idea to analyze and tokenize the city, state, and country, because it's more preferable to match these fields with the exact match than a partial or stemmed match that'll most likely return the undesired results. Another usage for `StringField` is the product model number, phone number, category, and so on.

How to do it...

Adding a `StringField` , a Field object that stores attribute,to a document is very easy. Here is a sample code on how it's done:

```
Document document = new Document();
document.add(new StringField("telephone_number", "04735264927",
  Field.Store.YES));
document.add(new StringField("area_code", "0484",
  Field.Store.YES));
indexWriter.addDocument(document);
indexWriter.commit();
```

How it works...

In this example, we created a `StringField` named telephone number to store the telephone number of a user. The `04735264927` value will be indexed as a single token. So, a query seeking an exact match of the telephone number will work fine in this case. Also, note the `Field.Store.Yes` option. We can control whether the field value should be stored or not. If you do not want to store the field you can use `Field.Store.No`. You can still sort by this field, but this value may not be included in the search results in this case.

The creation of a StringField is straightforward. We just need to specify the field type as StringField at the time of adding documents to the index. The options to store the field or not is also applicable in the case of a StringField.

Creating a TextField

Don't be confused between a StringField and TextField. Although both the fields contain textual data, there are major differences between these two fields. A StringField is not tokenized and it's a good tool for exact match and sorting. A TextField is tokenized and it's useful for storing any unstructured text for indexing. When you pass the text into an Analyzer for indexing, a TextField is what's used to store the text content.

How to do it...

Similar to the way in which a StringField is set, adding a TextField is also very straightforward. Let's review how it's done:

```
Document document = new Document();
String text = "Lucene is an Information Retrieval library
    written in Java.";
doc.add(new TextField("text", text, Field.Store.YES));
indexWriter.addDocument(document);
indexWriter.commit();
```

How it works...

This is a very simple example showing how a TextField is added, assuming that you have an Analyzer already created for the IndexWriter on the `text` field. The analysis process will run against this field to index the content within.

Creating a numeric field

We've learned how to deal with textual content using a StringField and TextField in Lucene, so now let's take a look at how numerals are handled. Lucene provides four Field classes for storing numeric values. They are IntField, FloatField, LongField, and DoubleField, and are analogous to Java numeric types. Lucene, being a text search engine, treats numeral as term internally and indexes them in a trie structure (also called ordered tree data structure) as illustrated in the following:

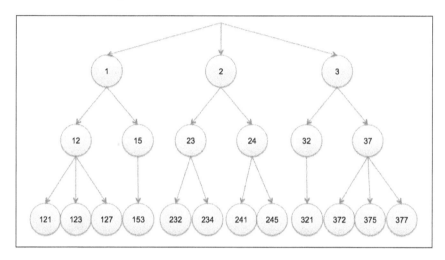

Each Term is logically assigned to larger and larger predefined lower-precision brackets. For example, let's assume that the brackets are divided by a quotient of division of a lower level by ten as in the preceding diagram. So, under the **1** bracket (at the top level), we get DocId associated with values in the *100s* range, and under the **12** bracket, we get association with values in the *120s* range and so on. Now, let's say you want to search by numeric range of all documents with the numeric value between *230* and *239*: Lucene can simply find the **23** bracket in the index and return all the DocIds underneath. As you can see, this technique allows Lucene to leverage its indexing power to also handle numerals with ease.

The numbers of brackets can be tuned by changing the value called **precisionStep**. A smaller precisionStep value will result in a larger number of brackets that will consume more disk space and, at the same time, will improve the search range performance. The value can only be changed by creating a FieldType custom. The default value is *4* and is selected by Lucene's team for a reasonable tradeoff between disk space consumption and performance.

Numeral values in Lucene can be sorted, searched by range, and matched exactly, which is similar to what you would do in a text field. Note that if you intend to sort by a numeric field, you should create a separate single-value field to sort purposes (by setting precisionStep to Integer.MAX_VALUE), as this is more efficient than using thebracketed index.

How to do it...

Let's look at a code sample for creating numeric fields:

```
IntField intField = new IntField("int_value", 100, Field.Store.YES);
LongField longField = new LongField("long_value", 100L, Field.Store.
YES);
FloatField floatField = new FloatField("float_value", 100.0F, Field.
Store.YES);
DoubleField doubleField = new DoubleField("double_value", 100.0D,
Field.Store.YES);
FieldType sortedIntField = new FieldType();
sortedIntField.setNumericType(FieldType.NumericType.INT);
sortedIntField.setNumericPrecisionStep(Integer.MAX_VALUE);
sortedIntField.setStored(false);
sortedIntField.setIndexed(true);
IntField intFieldSorted = new IntField("int_value_sort", 100,
sortedIntField);
Document document = new Document();
document.add(intField);
document.add(longField);
document.add(floatField);
document.add(doubleField);
document.add(intFieldSorted);
```

How it works...

The instantiation of different numeric fields are pretty much the same as you find in the code. The first parameter is the name of the field, the second parameter is the value, and last the parameter is `FieldType`. In our example, we specified that we want the field value stored by passing in `Field.Store.YES`.

In the second portion, where we defined our own `FieldType`, we can see a demonstration of creating a single-valued `IntField` to sort purposes. We set the numeric type to `FieldType.NumericType.INT` and `precisionStep` to `Integer.MAX_VALUE`, so that we can ensure the index is not bracketed. Then, we set stored to false because we are already storing the same `int` value in `intField`, and have indexed this to true so that this field goes into an index. Also, lastly, we created another Field called `intFieldSorted` to use this custom `FieldType`.

The fields are now ready to add to a document as shown in the last portion of the code.

Creating a DocValue Field

Similar to a stored field, DocValue is a part of a document. It's also created at indexing time, and contains value that are specific to a document. The major difference between the two concerns their underlying storage structure. The field's storage is row-oriented, whereas DocValue's storage is column-oriented. In retrieval, all field values are returned at once per document, so that loading the relevant information about a document is very fast. However, if you need to scan a field for any other purpose it will be a slow process, as you will have to iterate through all the documents and load each document's fields per iteration. The DocValue is stored by column in DocId to value mapping, and loading the values for a specific DocValue for all documents at once can be done quickly, as Lucene only has to scan through one column rather than iterating through each document to load a field. In summary, the field and DocValue both contain information about a document, but they serve a different purpose in practical usage.

The following is an illustration of how field and DocValue differ in a storage structure:

Field (row-oriented)

DocId: 1	Name: John	Gender: M	Age: 30
DocId: 2	Name: Mary	Gender: F	Age: 25
DocId: 3	Name: Peter	Gender: M	Age: 40

DocValue (column-oriented)

Name		Gender		Age	
DocId	Value	DocId	Value	DocId	Value
1	John	1	M	1	30
2	Mary	2	F	2	25
3	Peter	3	M	3	40

Lucene provides the following DocValue types:

- `BinaryDocValues`: This is a per-document byte[] array that can be used to store custom data structure
- `NumericDocValues`: This is a per-document single-valued numeric type value
- `SortedDocValues`: This is a per-document single-valued string type that's stored and sorted separately; the DocValue itself is a DocId to term ID mapping where the term ID references a term in a sorted term list
- `SortedNumericDocValues`: This is similar to `SortedDocValues`, but this is for numeric values only
- `SortedSetDocValues`: This is similar to `SortedDocValues`, but each document in DocValues is mapped to a set instead of a single value

How to do it...

Let's do an exercise to create and retrieve DocValues:

```
Analyzer analyzer = new StandardAnalyzer();
Directory directory = new RAMDirectory();
IndexWriterConfig config = new
  IndexWriterConfig(Version.LATEST, analyzer);
IndexWriter indexWriter = new IndexWriter(directory, config);
Document document = new Document();
document.add(new SortedDocValuesField("sorted_string", new
  BytesRef("hello")));
indexWriter.addDocument(document);
document = new Document();
document.add(new SortedDocValuesField("sorted_string", new
  BytesRef("world")));
indexWriter.addDocument(document);
indexWriter.commit();
indexWriter.close();
IndexReader reader = DirectoryReader.open(directory);
document = reader.document(0);
System.out.println("doc 0: " + document.toString());
document = reader.document(1);
System.out.println("doc 1: " + document.toString());
for (AtomicReaderContext context : reader.leaves()) {
  AtomicReader atomicReader = context.reader();
  SortedDocValues sortedDocValues =
    DocValues.getSorted(atomicReader, "sorted_string");
  System.out.println("Value count: " +
    sortedDocValues.getValueCount());
    System.out.println("doc 0 sorted_string: " +
  sortedDocValues.get(0).utf8ToString());
  System.out.println("doc 1 sorted_string: " +
    sortedDocValues.get(1).utf8ToString());
}

reader.close();
```

How it works...

The initial setup is very familiar. We obtain an IndexWriter by setting up an Analyzer object `StandardAnalyzer` and a Directory object `RAMDirectory`. Then, we add two documents with a single DocValues called `SortedDocValues` and no field. Note that we add a `SortedDocValues` by using `SortedDocValuesField`, which is similar to adding a regular field. For `SortedDocValuesField`, a String value needs to be converted to a bytes array by using `BytesRef`. After DocValues are added, we commit the changes and close the `IndexWriter`. We then open it with an `IndexReader`: a Reader that reads index data. Note that there are two print statements, which show that we have two documents in the index. Because the DocValues reader can only leverage `AtomicReader`, we need to iterate through all `AtomicReader` in `IndexReader`, in order to examine all the segments. An `AtomicReader` can only read one index segment, hence, the iteration. With `AtomicReader`, we can extract DocValues from `SortedDocValues` by calling `getSorted(AtomicReader, String)`. The next line shows that you can get a count of values in DocValues. The following two lines show that you can obtain DocValue by DocId. Here is the output from the sample code:

```
doc 0: Document<>
doc 1: Document<>
Value count: 2
doc 0 sorted_string: hello
doc 1 sorted_string: world
```

Transactional commits and index versioning

In the world of data management platforms, anything that supports transactional commits would implement **ACID** (**Atomicity, Consistency, Isolation, Durability**). ACID is a set of properties that guarantees that transactions are processed reliably. So, how does Lucene measure against ACID?

- **Atomicity**: This property requires that each transaction is *all or nothing*. When a transaction fails, none of the partial changes performed by the transaction should persist or be visible. Changes from a transaction should only persist and made visible when the transaction completes and is committed. Lucene's IndexWriter supports transactional commit. Changes to the index will only be made visible to `IndexReader` after we call `commit()`. If an IndexWriter crashes for whatever reason or never calls `commit()`, the partial changes will never be made visible to the IndexReader.

- **Consistency**: This property ensures that any committed changes will bring the system from one valid state to another valid state. Any changes written to the disk must be valid and conform to constraints, format, and any other rules that ensure the validity of the data. Lucene fully supports this property as the index is always valid and the uncommitted transactions will never be made visible. Lucene's index can survive crashes, a power failure, and even when the process itself is killed.

- **Isolation**: This property ensures that the concurrent execution of transactions is supported and that each transaction runs under its own isolation, without interfering with each other. Lucene handles this with an IndexWriter by not exposing the changes to the IndexReader during a transaction (before commit() is called).

- **Durability**: This property ensures that the changes remain intact once committed. Anything that's committed should survive crashes, a power failure, and so on. Lucene supports this by guaranteeing that when commit() is called, the changes from a transaction are persisted on the disk, so that any immediate failure after commit would not undo or alter the changes made through the transaction.

Lucene supports a two-phase commit where you can call prepareCommit() in IndexWriter to do all the necessary work (and flush the changes to the disk) beforehand. Then, you can call commit() to commit the changes or rollback() to rollback the transaction. Note that calling rollback() will also close the IndexWriter. Calling commit() actually triggers a call to prepareCommit() internally and calling close() will trigger a call to commit() before IndexWriter is closed.

A Lucene index may have multiple IndexCommits. Each IndexCommit can be considered as a point-in-time snapshot of the index. By default, Lucene uses a policy class called IndexDeletionPolicy that would delete prior IndexCommits after a successful commit. To keep previous IndexCommits, we will need to customize a IndexDeletionPolicy or use the built-in NoDeletionPolicy. Here is a list of IndexDeletionPolicy provided out of the box:

- KeepOnlyLastCommitDeletionPolicy: This keeps the most recent IndexCommit and immediately removes the prior IndexCommits after a new commit is complete. This is the default policy. This policy keeps the index directory tidy by removing old commits and gives you one possible rollback by keeping the last commit.

- NoDeletionPolicy: All the IndexCommits are kept. They are not removed until delete() is called on each IndexCommit. This policy is especially useful if it's important to provide a way to search the index in prior commits and maintain a set of rollback points. One possible use case is data reconciliation where you may need to perform a rollback when the data between data source and index are out of sync.

- ► SnapshotDeletionPolicy: A snapshot can be taken immediately after a commit. When a snapshot is held on an IndexCommit, it cannot be removed. A snapshotted IndexCommit can only be removed when the snapshot is released. This policy maintains snapshots in memory only. Note that this class is a wrapper class of another IndexDeletionPolicy class. This policy is useful for taking a hot backup of the index directory. While the snapshot is held, an external backup process can copy the index files to a backup location.

- ► PersistentSnapshotDeletionPolicy: This is similar to SnapshotDeletionPolicy; instead of keeping snapshots in memory, this policy persists snapshots on the disk in the same directory where the index resides. This policy is useful when you want to make sure a snapshot can survive against a system failure so a hot backup can be taken even after a failure.

How to do it...

We will demonstrate commit, rollback, and usage of IndexDeletionPolicy:

```
Analyzer analyzer = new StandardAnalyzer();
Directory directory = new RAMDirectory();
IndexWriterConfig config = new
  IndexWriterConfig(Version.LATEST, analyzer);
SnapshotDeletionPolicy policy = new
  SnapshotDeletionPolicy(NoDeletionPolicy.INSTANCE);
config.setIndexDeletionPolicy(policy);
IndexWriter indexWriter = new IndexWriter(directory, config);
IndexCommit lastSnapshot;
Document document = new Document();
indexWriter.addDocument(document);
indexWriter.commit();
lastSnapshot = policy.snapshot();
document = new Document();
indexWriter.addDocument(document);
indexWriter.commit();
lastSnapshot = policy.snapshot();
document = new Document();
indexWriter.addDocument(document);
indexWriter.rollback();
indexWriter.close();
List<IndexCommit> commits =
  DirectoryReader.listCommits(directory);
```

```
       System.out.println("Commits count: " + commits.size());
       for (IndexCommit commit : commits) {
          IndexReader reader = DirectoryReader.open(commit);
          System.out.println("Commit " + commit.getSegmentCount());
          System.out.println("Number of docs: " + reader.numDocs());
       }

       System.out.println("\nSnapshots count: " +
          policy.getSnapshotCount());
       List<IndexCommit> snapshots = policy.getSnapshots();
       for (IndexCommit snapshot : snapshots) {
          IndexReader reader = DirectoryReader.open(snapshot);
          System.out.println("Snapshot " +
             snapshot.getSegmentCount());
          System.out.println("Number of docs: " + reader.numDocs());
       }
       policy.release(lastSnapshot);
       System.out.println("\nSnapshots count: " +
          policy.getSnapshotCount());
```

How it works...

In this demonstration, we first set up a policy for deletion called `SnapshotDeletionPolicy` that wraps around `NoDeletionPolicy`. This means that all the commits are kept and the prior commits will not be removed automatically. Then, we start adding a document to the index, and committing and taking snapshots in between. Note that on the third document, we call rollback to rollback the changes and we use DirectoryReader to list all the past commits and `SnapshotDeletionPolicy` to list all the past snapshots.

The first print statement *Commits count* will output two because we added two documents and roll backed the third one. In the first iteration, you will find two commits. First commit should show *1* document and the second commit should show *2* documents. In the snapshot's iteration, it should show *2* snapshots with the similar output. At last, after we release a snapshot of one of the commits, the snapshot count should change to *1*.

The output of the code is as follows:

```
Commits count: 2
Commit 1
Number of docs: 1
Commit 2
Number of docs: 2
```

```
Snapshots count: 2
Snapshot 1
Number of docs: 1
Snapshot 2
Number of docs: 2

Snapshots count: 1
```

Reusing field and document objects per thread

Performance has always been a part of the main focus of Lucene's development team. Because they are adamant about achieving high efficiency and performance, we have all benefitted from this. To ensure that users can properly leverage Lucene's speed and efficiency, there are best practices that we should adhere to so that we don't introduce unnecessary inefficiency. One of the best practices is to reuse both the Document and field objects. This minimizes the object creation cost during any massive data import operations. It will also reduce the chance of triggering garbage collection.

There are a couple things to keep in mind when reusing Document object: we need to make sure that we clear out all the fields before putting in the new values; for the field, we can just simply overwrite the value.

How to do It...

Here is a sample code snippet on Document and field reuse:

```
Analyzer analyzer = new StandardAnalyzer();
Directory directory = new RAMDirectory();
IndexWriterConfig config = new
    IndexWriterConfig(Version.LATEST, analyzer);
IndexWriter indexWriter = new IndexWriter(directory, config);

Document doc = new Document();
StringField stringField = new StringField("name", "",
    Field.Store.YES);

String[] names = {"John", "Mary", "Peter"};
for (String name : names) {
    stringField.setStringValue(name);
    doc.removeField("name");
```

```
    doc.add(stringField);
    indexWriter.addDocument(doc);
  }

  indexWriter.commit();
  IndexReader reader = DirectoryReader.open(directory);
  for (int i = 0; i < 3; i++) {
    doc = reader.document(i);
    System.out.println("DocId: " + i + ", name: " +
      doc.getField("name").stringValue());
  }
```

How it works...

Note that both Document and StringField are only declared once and they are reused within the For loop. Inside the loop, the "name" Field is removed before being added. This is done so that we don't inherit the Field values from the previous iteration. The output of the code should be as follows:

```
DocId: 0, name: John
DocId: 1, name: Mary
DocId: 2, name: Peter
```

Delving into field norms

A norm is part of the calculation of a score that's used to measure relevancy. When we search, a score is calculated for each matching result. This score will then be used to sort the end results. The score is what we refer to as a relevancy score.

Norms are calculated per indexed Field. This is a product of index time calculation (based on TFIDFSimilarity) and lengthNorm (a calculated factor that favors a shorter document). The higher value can help boost the relevancy of a document, which means that the document will rank higher in search results.

To further influence the search results relevancy, Lucene allows for two types of boosting: index time boost and query time boost. Index time boost is set per indexed field. It can be used to promote documents based on certain field values. Query time boost can be set per query clause so that all the documents matched by it are multiplied by the boost. It's useful if a certain filter takes precedence over everything else.

Norms are stored compressed in a highly lossy, single-byte format. This is mainly done to minimize storage and conserve memory consumption. Also, it's not meant for comparing minute details, but for big differences between documents, where relevancy differences are more obvious.

For certain fields, such as the single-valued field, norms may not provide any added benefits. In such a case, you an omit the norms by customizing a fieldType. Unless memory consumption is an issue, normally, you can leave it alone.

How to do it...

Let's take a look at how boosting a norm can influence the results:

```java
Analyzer analyzer = new StandardAnalyzer();
Directory directory = new RAMDirectory();
IndexWriterConfig config = new
    IndexWriterConfig(Version.LATEST, analyzer);
IndexWriter indexWriter = new IndexWriter(directory, config);

Document doc = new Document();
TextField textField = new TextField("name", "",
    Field.Store.YES);

float boost = 1f;
String[] names = {"John R Smith", "Mary Smith", "Peter
    Smith"};
for (String name : names) {
    boost *= 1.1;
    textField.setStringValue(name);
    textField.setBoost(boost);
    doc.removeField("name");
    doc.add(textField);
    indexWriter.addDocument(doc);
}
indexWriter.commit();

IndexReader indexReader = DirectoryReader.open(directory);
IndexSearcher indexSearcher = new IndexSearcher(indexReader);
Query query = new TermQuery(new Term("name", "smith"));
TopDocs topDocs = indexSearcher.search(query, 100);
System.out.println("Searching 'smith'");
for (ScoreDoc scoreDoc : topDocs.scoreDocs) {
    doc = indexReader.document(scoreDoc.doc);
    System.out.println(doc.getField("name").stringValue());
}
```

How it works...

In this example, we are adding three documents with the name Field being indexed as TextField. We set a boost on the Field by 1.1 on each iteration, so *Peter Smith* will have the highest boost, then *Mary Smith*, and finally *John R Smith*. Then, we do a search on *smith* and print out the results.

If you run this code as-is, you will see the following results:

```
Searching 'smith'
Peter Smith
Mary Smith
John R Smith
```

This is as expected because the results are sorted based on the boost values, where `Peter Smith` has the highest boost. Try comment out `textField.setBoost(boost);` and run this again. The results should look like the following:

```
Searching 'smith'
Mary Smith
Peter Smith
John R Smith
```

Note that the order has changed. This order is not random: it's based on a default norms calculation where the length of the field is considered. In this scenario, because all three documents are matching the term `smith`, the major factor in the relevancy score calculation is left to length.

Changing similarity implementation used during indexing

Part of the norms calculation at the index time on is similarity. Lucene has already implemented a complex model called TFIDFSimilarity as a default calculation for norms; you can read more about it on Lucene's website. In this section, we will talk about how we can tune similarity to suit our needs.

We will go through a similar scenario as we used in our example in norms. Instead of using boost to influence relevancy, we will leverage a NumericDocValuesField called ranking that will act as our boost. We will show you how to pull NumericDocValues at a query time within a Similarity class and how we can use it to influence score. This exercise will give you an idea of what you can do with similarity customization.

Getting ready

To start writing your own Similarity class, you can begin by extending Similarity. Then, you can register your new class by simply calling `IndexWriterConfig.setSimilarity(Similarity)` in indexing and `IndexSearcher.setSimilarity(Similarity) in searching.`

How to do it...

Let's start with our own `Similarity` class:

```
public class MySimilarity extends Similarity {
  private Similarity sim = null;
  public MySimilarity(Similarity sim) {
    this.sim = sim;
  }
  @Override
  public long computeNorm(FieldInvertState state) {
    return sim.computeNorm(state);
  }
  @Override
  public Similarity.SimWeight computeWeight(float
    queryBoost,CollectionStatistics collectionStats,
      TermStatistics... termStats) {
    return sim.computeWeight(queryBoost, collectionStats,
      termStats);
  }
  @Override
  public Similarity.SimScorer
    simScorer(Similarity.SimWeight weight,
      AtomicReaderContext context)
  throws IOException {
    final Similarity.SimScorer scorer =
      sim.simScorer(weight, context);
    final NumericDocValues values =
      context.reader().getNumericDocValues("ranking");
    return new SimScorer() {
      @Override
      public float score(int i, float v) {
        return values.get(i) * scorer.score(i, v);
      }
```

```
            @Override
            public float computeSlopFactor(int i) {
              return scorer.computeSlopFactor(i);
            }
            @Override
            public float computePayloadFactor(int i, int i1,
              int i2, BytesRef bytesRef) {
            return scorer.computePayloadFactor(i, i1, i2,
              bytesRef);
            }
        };
    }
  }
```

This is our own Similarity class called `MySimilarity`. It extends from Similarity, and we need to implement three methods: `computeNorm`, `computeWeight`, and `simScorer`. We will focus on `simScorer` in this example as it provides a reference to `AtomicReader`, which we can use to pull DocValues. The constructor of this class accepts a Similarity class so that we can pass in an existing similarity implementation, such as `DefaultSimilarity`, as our default calculation since we only want to augment the results, not implement the calculation from scratch.

In the `simScorer` implementation, we pull `NumericDocValues` from `AtomicReader` so that it can be used by our own `simScorer`. We alter the score calculation by multiplying the score with the **ranking** value:

```
Here is the second portion of our example:
    Analyzer analyzer = new StandardAnalyzer();
    Directory directory = new RAMDirectory();
    IndexWriterConfig config = new IndexWriterConfig(Version.LATEST,
analyzer);
    MySimilarity similarity = new MySimilarity(new
DefaultSimilarity());
    config.setSimilarity(similarity);
    IndexWriter indexWriter = new IndexWriter(directory, config);

    Document doc = new Document();
    TextField textField = new TextField("name", "", Field.Store.YES);
    NumericDocValuesField docValuesField = new NumericDocValuesField(
"ranking", 1);
```

```
long ranking = 11;
String[] names = {"John R Smith", "Mary Smith", "Peter Smith"};
for (String name : names) {
    ranking *= 2;
    textField.setStringValue(name);
    docValuesField.setLongValue(ranking);
    doc.removeField("name");
    doc.removeField("ranking");
    doc.add(textField);
    doc.add(docValuesField);
    indexWriter.addDocument(doc);
}

indexWriter.commit();

IndexReader indexReader = DirectoryReader.open(directory);
IndexSearcher indexSearcher = new IndexSearcher(indexReader);
indexSearcher.setSimilarity(similarity);
Query query = new TermQuery(new Term("name", "smith"));
TopDocs topDocs = indexSearcher.search(query, 100);
System.out.println("Searching 'smith'");
for (ScoreDoc scoreDoc : topDocs.scoreDocs) {
    doc = indexReader.document(scoreDoc.doc);
    System.out.println(doc.getField("name").stringValue());
}
```

Note that this portion is very similar to the norms example. We instantiate MySimilarity at the top, and then we pass it into IndexWriterConfig and later to IndexSearcher. We are also adding a `NumericDocValues` ranking to each document where the value doubles in each iteration. The end result is as expected as follows, where the order is reversed:

```
Searching 'smith'
Peter Smith
Mary Smith
John R Smith
```

4

Searching Your Indexes

In this chapter, we will cover the following recipes:

- Obtaining IndexReaders
- Un-inverting single-valued fields in memory with FieldCache
- TermVectors
- IndexSearcher
- Constructing queries
- Specifying sort logic
- Forming a search result
- Pagination
- Using Collectors
- Sorting with custom FieldComparator

Introduction

So far, we have focused on indexing data and explored both the indexing and analysis processes in great detail. As you may expect, in a search application, both indexing and searching processes are equally important. In this chapter, we will look into search to give you a perspective on Lucene's capability and expandability nature.

Obtaining IndexReaders

As we have seen already, there are several prerequisites (for example, opening a directory, setting up an analyzer, and writing to index) to prepare an index for a search. Lucene provides the `IndexReader` class to access a point-in-time view of an index. It means that you can concurrently write to an index, while an existing `IndexReader` is reading without exposing any uncommitted data to the active `IndexReader`. This is an important concept to keep in mind because this architecture allows the possibility of providing a seamless transition between index versions by opening a new IndexReader while the old `IndexReader` is still servicing a search. The `DirectoryReader` is a subclass of `IndexReader`, which is the class that provides the facility to actually open a directory containing an index, and returns an `IndexReader`. DirectoryReader also has a more optimized index opening method called `openIfChanged` that will reuse the existing DirectoryReader for faster reopening of an index.

`IndexReader`, by itself, is an abstract class. It has two implementations: `AtomicReader` and `CompositeReader`. This `AtomicReader` is a single reader that's atomic for a single segment of an index that supports retrieval of stored fields, doc values, terms, and postings. This `CompositeReader` contains a list of `AtomicReaders` on multiple segments. It supports retrieval of stored fields only because the other properties (for example, norm values and doc values) need to be merged from the underlying `AtomicReaders`. It's up to the programmer to code facility classes by iterating through `CompositeReader.leaves()` to merge the results, or use a built-in class called `SlowCompositeReaderWrapper` to do the merge, although it has a significant performance hit from scanning the underlying `AtomicReaders`.

In our example, we will be using `DirectoryReader` to open an index. Note that `DirectoryReader` is an implementation of `CompositeReader`, so by calling its open method, it will return a `CompositeReader`.

How to do it...

Let's take a look at how we can obtain `IndexReader`:

```
// open a directory
Directory directory = FSDirectory.open(
    new File("/data/index"));
// set up a DirectoryReader
DirectoryReader directoryReader =
    DirectoryReader.open(directory);
// pull a list of underlying AtomicReaders
List<AtomicReaderContext> atomicReaderContexts =
    directoryReader.leaves();
// retrieve the first AtomicReader from the list
AtomicReader atomicReader =
```

```
        atomicReaderContexts.get(0).reader();
    // open another DirectoryReader by calling openIfChanged
    DirectoryReader newDirectoryReader =
        DirectoryReader.openIfChanged(directoryReader);
    // assign newDirectoryReader
    if (newDirectoryReader != null) {
        IndexSearcher indexSearcher =
            new IndexSearcher(newDirectoryReader);
        // close the old DirectoryReader
        directoryReader.close();
    }
```

How it works...

Note again that we obtained a `DirectoryReader` (essentially, an `IndexReader`) by calling `DirectoryReader.open(Directory)`. To gain access to the `AtomicReader` underneath, we need to call the `leaves()` method to retrieve a list of `AtomicReaderContext`, and from `AtomicReaderContext`, we can access `AtomicReader`. After we gain access to an `AtomicReader`, we have a demonstration of calling `openIfChanged(IndexReader)`. This call will return a new `DirectoryReader` if there is a change to the index. It returns null if the index has not changed.

Un-inverting single-valued fields in memory with FieldCache

We have learned very early on that Lucene stores data in an inverted index in which terms are sorted and DocId is associated with each term. A search is essentially finding DocId's intersection in matched terms. The index itself allows for a very fast term lookup, but it's not ideal for lookup by DocId. To solve the problem of finding a field value by DocId, Lucene introduced `FieldCache`. FieldCache is an in-memory data structure that stored in an array format in which the value position corresponds to DocId (since DocId is basically an ordinal value of all documents). Because each array position can only store one value, FieldCache should be used on single-valued fields only. In essence, Lucene uninverts data from the index and stores them in FieldCache.

 Note that when `FieldCache` is initialized, it stays static and it does not synchronize with `IndexReader`. If you need to reopen `IndexReader`, `FieldCache` will need to be reinitialized in order to be in sync with the latest changes.

How to do it...

Let's take a look at how `FieldCache` is set up:

```
StandardAnalyzer analyzer = new StandardAnalyzer();
Directory directory = new RAMDirectory();
IndexWriterConfig config =
    new IndexWriterConfig(Version.LATEST, analyzer);
IndexWriter indexWriter = new IndexWriter(directory, config);

Document doc = new Document();
StringField stringField =
    new StringField("name", "", Field.Store.YES);

String[] contents = {"alpha", "bravo", "charlie",
    "delta", "echo", "foxtrot"};
for (String content : contents) {
    stringField.setStringValue(content);
    doc.removeField("name");
    doc.add(stringField);
    indexWriter.addDocument(doc);
}

indexWriter.commit();

IndexReader indexReader = DirectoryReader.open(directory);

BinaryDocValues cache = FieldCache.DEFAULT.getTerms(
    SlowCompositeReaderWrapper.wrap(indexReader), "name", true);

for (int i = 0; i < indexReader.maxDoc(); i++) {
    BytesRef bytesRef = cache.get(i);
    System.out.println(i + ": " + bytesRef.utf8ToString());
}
```

How it works...

Here, we set up our index in a `RAMDirectory` using a `StandardAnalyzer`. The content we added to the index is an array of strings. To initialize FieldCache, we made a call to `FieldCache.DEFAULT.getTerms(AtomicReader, String, String)`. `FieldCache.DEFAULT` is a built-in singleton with the facilities to build and hold on to all the `FieldCache` we are initializing. In this sample code, we call the `getTerms` method to build a term-based `FieldCache`. Note that we wrap our `IndexReader` with a `SlowCompositeReaderWrapper` to simulate an `AtomicReader`, which is required to build FieldCache. The return object is a `BinaryDocValues` object, where we can retrieve a field value by DocId by calling the get method. We demonstrated this functionality by iterating the cache in a loop. This code should produce the following output:

```
0: alpha
1: bravo
2: charlie
3: delta
4: echo
5: foxtrot
```

TermVectors

`TermVectors` is a feature in Lucene that lets you retrieve per document term-based statistical data from the index. These additional data points can be useful for features such as highlighting or any term-based reports analysis. As you may expect, this feature is not enabled by default, as it can be expensive to compute these data points and it would increase the index size significantly.

This `TermVectors` provides the following additional data points for each document:

- Term frequency
- Term position(s)
- Term offsets

Term frequency is the number of times the term appears in a document. Positions is the term in a document where each position is incremented by term. offsets has a starting and ending positions by characters where the term can be located in a document.

Let's look at an example of what you can expect to see in `TermVectors`. Here is a piece of text to be added to a document:

```
humpty dumpty sat on a wall
```

Here is what you will retrieve from `TermVectors`:

Term	Frequency	Position	Offset
dumpty	1	1	[7,13]
humpty	1	0	[0,6]
sat	1	2	[14,17]
wall	1	5	[23,27]

Note that we omitted the terms *on* and *a* from the list, assuming that we used `StopWordFilter`.

How to do it...

Let's look at a code sample on how to set up and retrieve `TermVectors`:

```
StandardAnalyzer analyzer = new StandardAnalyzer();
Directory directory = new RAMDirectory();
IndexWriterConfig config =
        new IndexWriterConfig(Version.LATEST, analyzer);
IndexWriter indexWriter = new IndexWriter(directory, config);

FieldType textFieldType = new FieldType();
textFieldType.setIndexed(true);
textFieldType.setTokenized(true);
textFieldType.setStored(true);
textFieldType.setStoreTermVectors(true);
textFieldType.setStoreTermVectorPositions(true);
textFieldType.setStoreTermVectorOffsets(true);

Document doc = new Document();
Field textField = new Field("content", "", textFieldType);

String[] contents = {"Humpty Dumpty sat on a wall,",
        "Humpty Dumpty had a great fall.",
        "All the king's horses and all the king's men",
        "Couldn't put Humpty together again."};
```

```
for (String content : contents) {
    textField.setStringValue(content);
    doc.removeField("content");
    doc.add(textField);
    indexWriter.addDocument(doc);
}

indexWriter.commit();
IndexReader indexReader = DirectoryReader.open(directory);
DocsAndPositionsEnum docsAndPositionsEnum = null;
Terms termsVector = null;
TermsEnum termsEnum = null;
BytesRef term = null;
String val = null;

for (int i = 0; i < indexReader.maxDoc(); i++) {
    termsVector = indexReader.getTermVector(i, "content");
    termsEnum = termsVector.iterator(termsEnum);
    while ( (term = termsEnum.next()) != null ) {
        val = term.utf8ToString();
        System.out.println("DocId: " + i);
        System.out.println("  term: " + val);
        System.out.println("  length: " + term.length);
        docsAndPositionsEnum =
            termsEnum.docsAndPositions(null,
                docsAndPositionsEnum);
        if (docsAndPositionsEnum.nextDoc() >= 0) {
            int freq = docsAndPositionsEnum.freq();
            System.out.println("  freq: " +
                docsAndPositionsEnum.freq());
            for (int j = 0; j < freq; j++) {
                System.out.println("    [");
                System.out.println("      position: " +
                    docsAndPositionsEnum.nextPosition());
                System.out.println("      offset start: " +
                    docsAndPositionsEnum.startOffset());
                System.out.println("      offset end: " +
                    docsAndPositionsEnum.endOffset());
                System.out.println("    ]");
            }
        }
    }
}
```

How it works...

To enable `TermVectors`, we need to set up our own `FieldType` so we can turn on the `TermVectors` features. In our example, we enabled `TermVectors` on a text field that is analyzed by `StandardAnalyzer`. To retrieve the `TermVectors`, we called `getTermVectors` on `IndexReader` passing in a DocId and field name. This will return `TermVectors` for a particular document. Then, we iterate it using `TermsEnum` and retrieve the position and offset attributes with `DocsAndPositionsEnum`. In `TermsEnum`, we can retrieve terms and their length. In `DocsAndPositionsEnum`, we can retrieve term frequency, position(s), and offset. Note that the same term may appear multiple times in a document; hence, the second loop will iterate `DocsAndPositionsEnum`. Also, note that we need to call `nextPosition()` to iterate through `DocsAndPositionsEnum`.

Here is a code snippet of the output:

```
DocId: 0
  term: dumpty
  length: 6
  freq: 1
    [
      position: 1
      offset start: 7
      offset end: 13
    ]
DocId: 0
  term: humpty
  length: 6
  freq: 1
    [
      position: 0
      offset start: 0
      offset end: 6
    ]
```

Note that the terms are sorted alphabetically. `TermVector` stats can be found within the brackets.

IndexSearcher

Before we start a search, we need to obtain an `IndexSearcher` to help us facilitate the querying of an index. `IndexSearcher` provides a number of search methods for querying data and returning TopDocs as results. TopDocs represents hits from a search and contains an array of ScoreDoc where it contains DocId and the score of each matching document. Note that TopDocs contains DocId and does not actually contain any document content. Document content retrieval will have to be relied on `IndexReader` or `FieldCache`. An `IndexSearcher` requires an `IndexReader` as an input to its constructor to initialize.

How to do it...

Let's look at a simple code snippet to see how `IndexSearcher` is set up:

```
Directory directory =
    FSDirectory.open(new File("/data/index"));
DirectoryReader directoryReader =
    DirectoryReader.open(directory);
IndexSearcher indexSearcher =
    new IndexSearcher(directoryReader);
```

How it works...

First, we set up a Directory so that we can pass it onto a `DirectoryReader`, which is basically an `IndexReader`. Then, we pass the `DirectoryReader` to `IndexSearcher` for initialization. Note that `IndexReader` is fixated on a point-in-time snapshot of the index. If the index is updated, we need to make sure we reopen the `IndexReader` and `IndexSearcher` to expose the latest index changes to search.

Constructing queries

Now that we have an `IndexSearcher`, we are ready to proceed to querying. To begin, we will need to construct a `Query` object to pass into `IndexSearch`'s search method. There are a couple ways to construct a Query. Using a `QueryParser` class or constructing a Query programmatically, `QueryParser` provides the utility to interpret text and convert it into a Query. If you need to use search modifiers (for example, term must exist), there is a certain syntax to follow in order to form a query string. By default, a search phrase will return any documents that have matches on any of the query terms. We will demonstrate both `QueryParser` and constructing your own Query in this section.

Note that if you use `QueryParser`, you must also use an analyzer to analyze the query text.

How to do it...

Let's take a look at the following code snippets:

Code snippet 1:

```
Directory directory =
    FSDirectory.open(new File("/data/index"));
IndexReader indexReader =
    DirectoryReader.open(directory);
IndexSearcher indexSearcher =
    new IndexSearcher(indexReader);
Query query = new TermQuery(
    new Term("content", "alpha"));
TopDocs topDocs =
    indexSearcher.search(query, 100);
```

Code snippet 2:

```
Directory directory =
    FSDirectory.open(new File("/data/index"));
Analyzer analyzer = new StandardAnalyzer();
IndexReader indexReader =
    DirectoryReader.open(directory);
IndexSearcher indexSearcher =
    new IndexSearcher(indexReader);
QueryParser queryParser =
    new QueryParser("content", analyzer);
Query query = queryParser.parse("alpha beta");
TopDocs topDocs =
    indexSearcher.search(query, 100);
```

How it works...

In the first code snippet, we programmatically created a Query object by instantiating `TermQuery`. Note that we don't have any analyzer in this example. Because we are not parsing any string, we created a `TermQuery` directly for search.

In second code snippet, we leverage `QueryParser` to generate a Query object. In the `QueryParser` can accept any text and turn it into a Query. Note that we also need to provide an `Analyzer` to `QueryParser`. This is done so that we can apply the same text analysis treatment as in the indexing process, to ensure accuracy of the search.

Specifying sort logic

Lucene, by default, scores every search results and the results are sorted in descending order of the relevance scores. The scoring ensures that the most relevant results are shown before the less relevant ones. This generally works great for most applications. However, sometimes user may prefer to sort results based on other criteria. For example, in an e-commerce website, user may prefer to sort results by price. This type of a scenario brings us to the topic of specifying sort in Lucene.

To specify sort, we first need to create one or more `SortField` objects. Then, we create a sort object that wraps around `SortField(s)` to pass along to IndexSearcher's search method. The Sort class itself has two static Sort:

- ▸ **RELEVANCE**: This is sorting by relevance score, which is done by default (without specifying Sort).
- ▸ **INDEX ORDER**: This is sorting by index order, which is the natural order of the documents in the index.

The `SortField` class can be instantiated with a `Field` name and `SortField`.type. The types are the usual string and numeric types: `DOUBLE`, `FLOAT`, `INT`, and `LONG`. You can also sort by `BYTES` or `SCORE` (same as `Sort.RELEVANCE`). If you prefer to customize Sort, you may do so by providing your own comparator logic.

Sort is performed in memory and sorted field is stored in cache. From Lucene's documentation, the formula to estimate memory usage in Sort is as follows:

```
4 * IndexReader.maxDoc() * (# of different sort fields)
```

The cache itself is an array of integers of length `IndexReader.maxDoc()`. So, be mindful of memory consumption when you design your application.

How to do it...

Let's look at an example to see how Sort is specified:

```
StandardAnalyzer analyzer = new StandardAnalyzer();
Directory directory = new RAMDirectory();
IndexWriterConfig config = new IndexWriterConfig(Version.LATEST,
analyzer);
IndexWriter indexWriter = new IndexWriter(directory, config);

Document doc = new Document();
StringField stringField = new StringField("name", "", Field.Store.
YES);
```

```
String[] contents = {"foxtrot", "echo", "delta", "charlie", "bravo",
"alpha"};
for (String content : contents) {
    stringField.setStringValue(content);
    doc.removeField("name");
    doc.add(stringField);
    indexWriter.addDocument(doc);
}

indexWriter.commit();

IndexReader indexReader = DirectoryReader.open(directory);
IndexSearcher indexSearcher = new IndexSearcher(indexReader);
WildcardQuery query = new WildcardQuery(new Term("name","*"));
SortField sortField = new SortField("name", SortField.Type.STRING);
Sort sort = new Sort(sortField);

TopDocs topDocs = indexSearcher.search(query, null, 100, sort);
for (ScoreDoc scoreDoc : topDocs.scoreDocs) {
    doc = indexReader.document(scoreDoc.doc);
    System.out.println(scoreDoc.score + ": " + doc.getField("name").
stringValue());
}
```

How it works...

In this example, we add a list of words in reverse alphabetical order into an index. Then, we perform a wildcard search on * so that we match on everything. Next, we create a `SortField` on the `name` field (same as input) and wrap it in Sort. We perform a search right after, iterate through the results, and print the score and `name` field to `System.out`. Here is the output:

```
NaN: alpha
NaN: bravo
NaN: charlie
NaN: delta
NaN: echo
NaN: foxtrot
```

A couple of observations: there are no scores and the result is sorted alphabetically as we intended. We don't get any scores because we specified a Sort that doesn't involve scoring; hence, no need to compute scores. Also, had we not specified a Sort, the result would be in reverse order.

Forming a search result

By now, we have seen various examples of searches, but we haven't yet talked about search results in detail. Let's take a look at what we get in return when we perform a search. In `IndexSearcher`, there are several ways to submit a search. You can search by Query, with a Filter and Sort. You may notice that there is also an `int` field in which to specify the maximum number of results to return. This value is useful when you implement pagination. The return object from the search method is TopDocs. TopDocs has two attributes, an array of `ScoreDoc` and `totalHits`. The `ScoreDoc` contains DocId and score. `totalHits` is the total number of matching documents in this search. Note that the max results `int` value has no effect on `totalHits` as `totalHits` is the overall count of the matching documents.

As you may have noticed, the results returned from the search are just a list of pointers (DocId) and their scores. We don't actually get any document content from search. To retrieve the document content, we will have to resort to calling `IndexReader.document(int)` passing in DocId. This will return a document object. If a field is stored (`Field.Store.YES`), we can retrieve the field value from the index by calling `Document.getField(String)`. Alternatively, if the field values are stored in FieldCache, you can pull the value directly from `FieldCache` instead of pulling the document object (from a disk). Since `FieldCache` is in memory, it will be a lot faster than getting a field value from a document object.

How to do it...

Here is a demonstration of a simple search and document retrieval routine:

```
StandardAnalyzer analyzer = new StandardAnalyzer();
Directory directory = new RAMDirectory();
IndexWriterConfig config = new IndexWriterConfig(Version.LATEST,
analyzer);
IndexWriter indexWriter = new IndexWriter(directory, config);

Document doc = new Document();
TextField textField = new TextField("content", "", Field.Store.YES);

String[] contents = {"Humpty Dumpty sat on a wall,",
        "Humpty Dumpty had a great fall.",
        "All the king's horses and all the king's men",
        "Couldn't put Humpty together again."};
for (String content : contents) {
    textField.setStringValue(content);
    doc.removeField("content");
    doc.add(textField);
```

```
        indexWriter.addDocument(doc);
    }

    indexWriter.commit();

    IndexReader indexReader = DirectoryReader.open(directory);
    IndexSearcher indexSearcher = new IndexSearcher(indexReader);
    QueryParser queryParser = new QueryParser("content", analyzer);
    Query query = queryParser.parse("humpty dumpty");

    TopDocs topDocs = indexSearcher.search(query, 2);
    System.out.println("Total hits: " + topDocs.totalHits);
    for (ScoreDoc scoreDoc : topDocs.scoreDocs) {
        doc = indexReader.document(scoreDoc.doc);
        System.out.println(scoreDoc.score + ": " + doc.
getField("content").stringValue());
    }
```

How it works...

In this example, we are opening a `RAMDirectory` with a `StandardAnalyzer` and
indexing content in TextField. Then, we perform a simple search on the phrase `humpty`
`dumpty`. This should give us three hits. Here is what the results will look like:

```
Total hits: 3
0.81518793: Humpty Dumpty sat on a wall,
0.7132894: Humpty Dumpty had a great fall.
```

When you run the code, you will see that the total hits is 3, but the result listing will only
show 2 records. This is because we set the max results to 2 in the search method, which is in
`indexSearcher.search(query, 2)`.

Pagination

Traditionally, when you display results from a query (which can be expensive at times),
you may cache the results in memory and probably within a session only, so that you can
feed the results back to the user in piecemeal by iterating through the result. This is one
of the optimization techniques to minimize the number of queries to the search engine.
In Lucene, the preferable way of handling pagination is to perform separate searches per
page. Lucene's developers are confident enough that Lucene will perform well enough and
any potential performance issues will outweigh the complexity of implementing your own
pagination in memory.

One way to implement pagination is to use IndexSearcher's `searchAfter` method. It's similar to search with the addition of a ScoreDoc parameter in which the top results would return after the `ScoreDoc`. We can pass the last `ScoreDoc` of the previous page to `searchAfter`, so we can retrieve the following page.

How to do it...

Let's look at an example:

```
StandardAnalyzer analyzer = new StandardAnalyzer();
Directory directory = new RAMDirectory();
IndexWriterConfig config = new IndexWriterConfig(Version.LATEST,
  analyzer);
IndexWriter indexWriter = new IndexWriter(directory, config);
Document doc = new Document();
TextField textField = new TextField("content", "",
  Field.Store.YES);
String[] contents = {"Humpty Dumpty sat on a wall,",
    "Humpty Dumpty had a great fall.",
      "All the king's horses and all the king's men",
        "Couldn't put Humpty together again."};
for (String content : contents) {
    textField.setStringValue(content);
    doc.removeField("content");
    doc.add(textField);
    indexWriter.addDocument(doc);
}

indexWriter.commit();

IndexReader indexReader = DirectoryReader.open(directory);
IndexSearcher indexSearcher = new IndexSearcher(indexReader);
QueryParser queryParser = new QueryParser("content", analyzer);
Query query = queryParser.parse("humpty dumpty");
TopDocs topDocs = indexSearcher.search(query, 2);
ScoreDoc lastScoreDoc = null;
int page = 1;
System.out.println("Total hits: " + topDocs.totalHits);
while (true) {
    System.out.println("Page " + page);

    for (ScoreDoc scoreDoc : topDocs.scoreDocs) {
```

```
        doc = indexReader.document(scoreDoc.doc);
        System.out.println(scoreDoc.score + ": " + doc.
getField("content").stringValue());
        lastScoreDoc = scoreDoc;
    }
    topDocs = indexSearcher.searchAfter(lastScoreDoc, query, 2);
    if (topDocs.scoreDocs.length == 0) {
        break;
    }
    page++;
}
```

How it works...

This sample code demonstrates the use of the `searchAfter` method for pagination. After the initial search, we display the total hits. Then, we have a `while loop` with a break when TopDocs is empty. Inside the loop, we iterate through TopDocs and set the `lastSocreDoc` variable. After the loop, we pass `lastScoreDoc` to `searchAfter`. Note that the parameters are similar to what we sent to search previously. This call will return documents after `lastScoreDoc`. Here is what the results will look like:

```
Total hits: 3
Page 1
0.81518793: Humpty Dumpty sat on a wall,
0.7132894: Humpty Dumpty had a great fall.
Page 2
0.13417153: Couldn't put Humpty together again.
```

Our page size is essentially 2, so our results are broken down into two pages where page 1 has 2 results and page 2 has 1 result.

Using Collectors

Collector is an advanced feature that deals with the low-level handling of search results data. The implementation of this class is necessary to produce usable search results. When we call the `IndexSearcher.search` methods, we are actually already using Collector under the hood. So, what exactly is Collector? You can think of it as a refinery of search results after documents are matched. The matched documents are sent to Collector to score and sort. The default Collector we use in `IndexSearcher.search` is called `TopScoreDocCollector`. It scores documents using a scorer and sorts results based on the scores.

Normally, you shouldn't have to mess with Collector. However, on a rare occasion when you need more control over how the matched documents are scored, sorted, or even filtered, Collector can be a good place to work on the customization. This is assuming that you have already exhausted the options of custom filter, similarity, and/or analyzer.

How to do it...

Let's take a look how we build a custom Collector:

```
public class MyCollector extends Collector {
    private int totalHits = 0;
    private int docBase;
    private Scorer scorer;
    private List<ScoreDoc> topDocs = new ArrayList();
    private ScoreDoc[] scoreDocs;

    public MyCollector() { }

    public void setScorer(Scorer scorer) {
        this.scorer = scorer;
    }

    public boolean acceptsDocsOutOfOrder() {
        return false;
    }

    public void collect(int doc) throws IOException {
        float score = scorer.score();
        if (score > 0) {
            score += (1 / (doc + 1));
        }
        ScoreDoc scoreDoc =
            new ScoreDoc(doc + docBase, score);
        topDocs.add(scoreDoc);
        totalHits++;
    }

    public void setNextReader(AtomicReaderContext context) {
        this.docBase = context.docBase;
    }

    public int getTotalHits() {
        return totalHits;
    }

    public ScoreDoc[] getScoreDocs() {
        if (scoreDocs != null) {
            return scoreDocs;
        }
```

```
            Collections.sort(topDocs,
              new Comparator<ScoreDoc>() {
                public int compare(ScoreDoc d1, ScoreDoc d2) {
                    if (d1.score > d2.score) {
                        return -1;
                    } else if (d1.score == d2.score) {
                        return 0;
                    } else {
                        return 1;
                    }
                }
            });
            scoreDocs = topDocs.toArray(
                new ScoreDoc[topDocs.size()]);
            return scoreDocs;
        }
    }
```

Note that this sample code is meant to demonstrate the purpose only and it is by no means optimized. We simply used an `ArrayList` to store `ScoreDoc` and sorted it via Collections for illustration purposes only.

How it works...

In this example, we created our own Collector called `MyCollector`, extending from the Collector class. To implement this abstract class, we need to implement the following interfaces:

- ▶ `acceptsDocsOutOfOrder()`: This returns a Boolean value, indicating whether this Collector will accept a document out of order (by DocId).

- ▶ `collect(int)`: This is called once per matched document. This is where we can score the document and even filter out unwanted documents.

- ▶ `setNextReader(AtomicReaderContext)`: This is called before the Collector begins to collect from an AtomicReader.

- ▶ `setScorer(Scorer)`: This is called to put a `Scorer` in the Collector.

Sorting with custom FieldComparator

Besides building your own Collector to customize how the results are stored and sorted, another way to customize results sorting is to implement your own `FieldComparator` for `SortField`. Note that this customization only deals with the sorting aspect of the result set; it does not give you the flexibility to filter out results, as you would have with Collector.

To implement a `FieldComparator`, we need to implement two classes: `FieldComparator` and `FieldComparatorSource`. The `FieldComparator` is the underlying class that contains the methods for comparing the documents in the result set. The `FieldComparatorSource` is a class that instantiates `FieldComparator`. It acts like a wrapper on `FieldComparator`. To use it, we pass our own `FieldComparatorSource` in the place of `SortField.Type` into the constructor of `SortField`.

How to do it...

Let's take a look at how `FieldComparator` is implemented. We will build a custom `FieldComparator` to sort results on a single-valued field by length of the field value in and then by alphabetical order, both in ascending order:

```
public class MyFieldComparator extends
                        FieldComparator<String> {
    private String field;
    private String bottom;
    private String topValue;
    private BinaryDocValues cache;
    private String[] values;

    public MyFieldComparator(String field,
                             int numHits) {
        this.field = field;
        this.values = new String[numHits];
    }
    public int compare(int slot1, int slot2) {
        return compareValues(values[slot1],
                             values[slot2]);
    }
    public int compareBottom(int doc) {
        return compareValues(bottom,
                cache.get(doc).utf8ToString());
    }
}
```

```
       public int compareTop(int doc) {
           return compareValues(topValue,
                   cache.get(doc).utf8ToString());
       }
       public int compareValues(String first,
                                String second) {
           int val = first.length() - second.length();
           return val == 0 ?
                   first.compareTo(second) : val;
       }
       public void copy(int slot, int doc) {
           values[slot] = cache.get(doc).utf8ToString();
       }
       public void setBottom(int slot) {
           this.bottom = values[slot];
       }
       public void setTopValue(String value) {
           this.topValue = value;
       }
       public String value(int slot) {
           return values[slot];
       }
       public FieldComparator<String> setNextReader(
               AtomicReaderContext context)
               throws IOException {
           this.cache = FieldCache.DEFAULT.getTerms(
                           context.reader(), field, true);
           return this;
       }
   }
   public class MyFieldComparatorSource
                       extends FieldComparatorSource {
       public FieldComparator newComparator(
               String fieldname, int numHits,
               int sortPos, boolean reversed) {
           return new MyFieldComparator(fieldname, numHits);
       }
   }
```

How it works...

Note that there are a number of abstract methods to implement in `FieldComparator`. The key method in our implementation is `compareValues(String, String)`. This is where we actually compare values by length and then by alphabetical order. There are two kinds of references in the implementation: slot and doc. A slot references value relative to the returning result set. The reference is different from DocId and if there is pagination, a lot is in reference to the value in the current page. A doc is simply the DocId. We also hold on to a reference to `FieldCache` and it's set in `setNextReader` when `IndexReader` is passed into the `FieldComparator`. A field value is copied from `FieldCache` to slots in the copy method.

To use our own `MyFieldComparator`, we need to create our own `MyFieldComparatorSource` to instantiate our `FieldComparator`. `MyFieldComparatorSource` can be used to instantiate a `SortField`.

5
Near Real-time Searching

These are the recipes we are going to cover in this chapter:

▶ Using the DirectoryReader to open index in Near Real-time

▶ Using the SearcherManager to refresh IndexSearcher

▶ Generational indexing with TrackingIndexWriter

▶ Maintaining search sessions with SearcherLifetimeManager

▶ Performance tuning: latency and throughput

Introduction

In some search applications, it may be necessary to immediately expose any changes made to the index to attain the best user experience. For example, such applications can be forums where a user may search for his/her newly edited post to confirm that the submission is successful and see how it ranked in the search results. If the application is database-backed, post-edit searches will always be able to bring back the submitted post as index updates, and searches are mostly real-time in a single database environment, assuming reads and writes are on the same table. However, performance can take a toll if changes are frequent and the search volume is high because frequent updates can cause high IO load, which in turn contributes to performance issues. Performing a lot of searches on a frequently updated table is not ideal as collisions between read and write requests are bound to happen and updates can block read requests. The read requests backlog can queue up to a point where the application becomes unresponsive.

A natural progression in solving the locking issue is to introduce a read-only replica, so that we can offload reads to a different database environment, preventing updates and reads backlog on master database. It's possible to have many replicas so that the application can, in theory, scale horizontally and is limited by the amount of hardware only. One caveat with this approach is that we need to take extra precaution to prevent breaking the replication, because once the replication stops, replicas will slack behind and become stale quite quickly on a busy website. Also, a real-time search will not be consistent because of the potential delays in replication.

Lucene, as a high performance search engine, allows you to handle scale gracefully. We can multithread an application sharing the same IndexSearcher to scale up with as many CPU cores as we can get our hands on. We can also replicate the index into multiple machines so that we can spawn multiple searcher instances-though this will take some coordination to distribute index updates. Lucene also supports **Near Real-Time** (**NRT**) searching and it provides several utilities for handling NRT. Although the NRT feature is not exactly (or claimed to be) real-time, the latency between updates and searches can be set close enough so that searches will appear to the users as real-time. In this chapter, we will explore different ways of building an NRT search application. We will look into Lucene's NRT utility classes to learn about their purposes and see how to use them effectively.

Using the DirectoryReader to open index in Near Real-Time

First of all, let's cover the basics. The `DirectoryReader` attribute that we are already familiar with actually allows you to open an index with `IndexWriter` with the option to include uncommitted changes. This gives you a point-in-time snapshot of the index, including any updates that are not committed yet. In a typical search application, `IndexSearcher` would need to be reopened periodically anyway to expose recent updates. This feature provides an option to immediately expose index updates without waiting for `IndexWriter` to commit first. Potentially, the search application may have to maintain multiple `IndexSearchers` as depicted in the following diagram:

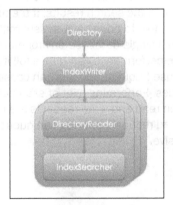

One use case for this feature is that users may want to review their recently submitted content to see how it ranked in search results. To provide the most up-to-date index after a user submits an update, we can open a new IndexSearcher with uncommitted changes to serve queries while the IndexWriter attribute committing changes in the background. A new IndexSearcher can be scheduled to reopen periodically after the IndexWriter commit, so we can keep search up to date. One caveat is that we will have to manage multiple IndexSearchers and ensure that each IndexSearcher is properly closed at the end of its lifecycle, so that we don't run into memory leaks issue.

How to do it...

Here is an example of using DirectoryReader to open an index in NRT:

```
Directory directory = FSDirectory.open(new File("data/index"));
StandardAnalyzer analyzer = new StandardAnalyzer();
IndexWriterConfig config = new IndexWriterConfig(Version.LATEST,
analyzer);
IndexWriter indexWriter = new IndexWriter(directory, config);

Document doc = new Document();
TextField textField = new TextField("content", "", Field.Store.YES);
String[] contents = {"Humpty Dumpty sat on a wall,",
        "Humpty Dumpty had a great fall.",
        "All the king's horses and all the king's men",
        "Couldn't put Humpty together again."};

for (String content : contents) {
    textField.setStringValue(content);
    doc.removeField("content");
    doc.add(textField);
    indexWriter.addDocument(doc);
}
DirectoryReader directoryReader =
DirectoryReader.open(indexWriter, true);
IndexSearcher indexSearcher = new IndexSearcher(directoryReader);

QueryParser queryParser = new QueryParser("content", analyzer);
Query query = queryParser.parse("humpty dumpty");

TopDocs topDocs = indexSearcher.search(query, 100);
for (ScoreDoc scoreDoc : topDocs.scoreDocs) {
    doc = indexSearcher.doc(scoreDoc.doc);
    System.out.println(scoreDoc.score + ": " +
      doc.getField("content").stringValue());
}
indexWriter.commit();
```

How it works...

We should be very familiar with this test setup, where we create a directory and IndexWriter to add a document to an index. One thing to take a note of in this example is that we perform a search before an index commit, which happens at the very end. You will be able to see the search results when you run this code, even though commit happens after the search. The key statement in this example is `DirectoryReader.open(indexWriter, true)`. Note that instead of passing in a Directory to `DirectoryReader`, we pass in an `IndexWriter` attribute. This allows `DirectoryReader` to merge uncommitted updates in `IndexWriter` to provide a coherent index. The second argument is a Boolean value that controls whether to apply all the outstanding deletes. The reason we are given an option as to whether to apply deletes is because when deleting documents, they are marked as deleted, but not removed from the index. Applying deletes will require some CPU cycles to clean up before the changes are exposed-hence the option. If you don't care about exposing recent deletes, you will gain better refresh timing by setting this Boolean value to false. Uncommitted updates are exposed as a single segment, so once the `DirectoryReader` attribute is opened to read uncommitted changes, the search application can function as usual, treating the `DirectoryReader` attribute in the same way as reading from a committed index.

This method is a simple way to achieve an NRT search. It demonstrates that the key component in NRT is IndexWriter. IndexWriter provides access to the index and outstanding changes that are stored in its buffer.

Using the SearcherManager to refresh IndexSearcher

The `SearcherManager` is a utility class that facilitates the sharing of `IndexSearcher` across multiple threads. It provides the facilities to **acquire** and **release** `IndexSearcher`, while allowing `IndexSearcher` to be reopened periodically. The `IndexSearcher` attribute can be refreshed by calling `maybeRefresh` prior to acquire, though it's recommended that this method be called periodically in a separate thread to minimize impacting a query that happens to trigger a refresh. Note that it's very important to call `release` so `SearcherManager` knows when `IndexSearcher` is not in use so that it can be closed for a refresh.

The following diagram shows SearcherManager's main responsibilities:

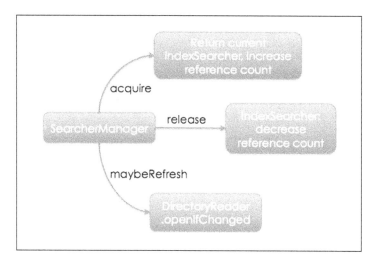

The `SearcherManager`'s constructor takes three arguments: an `IndexWriter`, a Boolean indicating whether to apply uncommitted deletes, and a `SearcherFactory`. In our example, we will use the built-in `SearcherFactory`. The `SearcherFactory` object can be extended to include custom configuration such as similarity, so when the `IndexSearcher` is refreshed, we don't lose any custom settings in the `IndexSearcher`.

When building a high traffics search application where both updates and searches are frequent, it is advisable to schedule index refreshes on a regular basis, perhaps every second, instead of on demand (after user submitted updates). This way, we can minimize the number of opened `IndexSearchers` and in turn, minimize memory consumption. With `SearcherManager`, we can call `maybeRefresh` in a separate thread to refresh the index in the background. The acquire and release methods encapsulate the logic of opening and closing `IndexSearcher` and will always return the latest `IndexSearcher`. At a one second refresh rate, the `IndexSearcher` will only be a second behind the real-time update. You can certainly adjust the refresh rate based on the requirement and available memory.

The benefit of using `SearcherManager` is that it handles the management of the `IndexSearcher` refreshes internally and lets you share a single `IndexSearcher` across multiple threads. The acquire method should always return an `IndexSearcher` so that it simplifies the instantiation logic.

How to do it...

Here is an example of using `SearcherManager`:

```
SearcherManager searcherManager = new SearcherManager(indexWriter,
true, new SearcherFactory());

// add documents to index here

searcherManager.maybeRefresh();
indexSearcher = searcherManager.acquire();

// perform search here

searcherManager.release(indexSearcher);

indexWriter.commit();

// add more documents to index here

searcherManager.maybeRefresh();
indexSearcher = searcherManager.acquire();

// perform search here

searcherManager.release(indexSearcher);

indexWriter.commit();
```

How it works...

In this example, we intentionally strip out the usual test setup so that we can highlight the important statements. Make a note of how we set up `SearcherManager` by passing in an `IndexWriter`, a true value (so we can read all the uncommitted deletes), and a default `SearcherFactory`. Before we perform a search, we call `maybeRefresh` to check whether there are any outstanding changes since `IndexSearcher` was last opened. In this case, because we haven't opened an `IndexSearcher` yet, this will trigger a refresh. Then, `IndexSearcher` is obtained by calling acquire. A search is performed and all the changes from above should be visible at this point. Then, we call commit to persist the changes. Note that we call release to tell the `SearcherManager` that we are done using the `IndexSearcher`. More documents are then added after commit, so another `maybeRefresh` and acquire is called to get a fresh `IndexSearcher`. The second search should include the newly added documents. Then, we call release and commit the changes at the end.

This is a very simple example that shows you what you can do with `SearcherManager`. In an actual implementation, you will most likely call `maybeRefresh` in a separate thread to avoid wasting CPU cycles in every query. Especially in a high-traffics application, calling `maybeRefresh` periodically on a schedule is preferable than calling it on every query request.

Generational indexing with TrackingIndexWriter

A generation is analogous to versioning in a revision control system. In TrackingIndexWriter, when an index changes, a new generation is created and can be used to open the index in that particular point in time. TrackingIndexWriter is a wrapper class to IndexWriter. It provides the corresponding `addDocument`, `updateDocument`, and `deleteDocument` methods to keep a track of index changes. On each update, a long value is returned, reflecting the current index generation. This value can be used to acquire an IndexSearcher that includes all the updates up to this specific point (generation). This class is intended to run alongside with `ControlledRealTimeReopenThread`. The `ControlledRealTimeReopenThread` is a utility class that runs as a separate thread managing the periodic reopening of the IndexSearcher. It accepts the `TrackingIndexWriter` and `SearcherManager` in its constructor to initialize this object. The generation value returned from `TrackingIndexWriter` can be used to tell `ControlledRealTimeReopenThread` to reopen index to a specific generation.

The relationship between components can be seen in the following diagram:

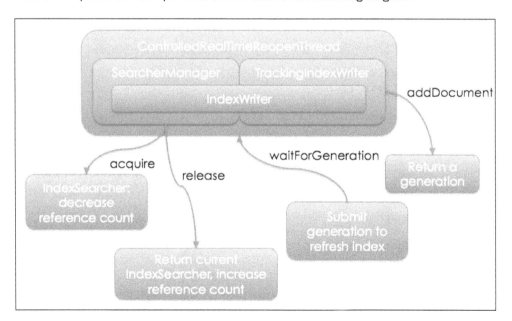

These utility classes can be used in conjunction with `SearcherManager`, with periodic index refreshes. The `ControlledRealTimeReopenThread` method provides the facility to refresh an index to a specific generation that guarantees inclusion of certain changes: say for a particular user after an update, while `SearcherManager` can trigger regular refreshes to maintain a general `IndexSearcher` freshness.

How to do it...

Here is the sample code on `TrackingIndexWriter`:

```
SearcherManager searcherManager = new SearcherManager(indexWriter,
true, new SearcherFactory());
TrackingIndexWriter trackingIndexWriter = new
TrackingIndexWriter(indexWriter);
ControlledRealTimeReopenThread controlledRealTimeReopenThread =
new ControlledRealTimeReopenThread(trackingIndexWriter,
searcherManager, 5, 0.001f);
controlledRealTimeReopenThread.start();

long indexGeneration = 0;

// add documents to index here

indexGeneration = trackingIndexWriter.addDocument(doc);

controlledRealTimeReopenThread.waitForGeneration(indexGeneration);
IndexSearcher indexSearcher = searcherManager.acquire();

// perform search here

searcherManager.release();
indexWriter.commit();

// add more documents to index here

indexGeneration = trackingIndexWriter.addDocument(doc);

controlledRealTimeReopenThread.waitForGeneration(indexGeneration);
indexSearcher = searcherManager.acquire();

// perform another search here

searcherManager.release();

controlledRealTimeReopenThread.close();
indexWriter.commit();
```

How it works...

Here, we instantiated a `SearcherManager` instance to pass along to
`TrackingIndexWriter`. Then, we pass both of these objects into
`ControlledRealTimeReopenThread` to instantiate it. Note that we keep a long value
`indexGeneration` to store the generation value on each index update (for example,
`addDocument`). We make a call to the `ControllerRealTimeReopenThread's`
`waitForGeneration` method with `indexGeneration`. This tells the thread to refresh
an index to the specified generation. When we call `searcherManager.acquire()` to
return an `IndexSearcher`, the `IndexSearcher` should include all the changes up to
the specified generation. You can also pass a maximum wait time (in milliseconds) to
`waitForGeneration` so that the thread will only wait up to the specified duration instead
of indefinitely. When the time is up and the index generation is not available, it will leave the
currently opened index as it is.

This mechanism is useful when there is a need to provide a search result to a specific point in
time. For example, a search right after a user submitted a post to a forum. This is especially,
useful when it's necessary to guarantee that certain changes be included in the search.

Maintaining search sessions with SearcherLifetimeManager

This is another utility class that Lucene provides out of the box, providing a facility to manage
multiple `IndexSearchers`. Why do we need multiple `IndexSearchers`? Let's imagine
we have multiple users in a high traffics NRT search application, searching concurrently.
Also, let's assume that some of these users are also submitting changes to the index at
the same time. If we periodically refresh our `IndexSearcher` for a NRT search, we will
likely encounter a scenario where a user is paginating through a result set and at the same
time, the index is updated affecting the search result. The effect can be minimal if the
newly added/updated content is irrelevant to the current search terms. However, if the new
content has any relevancy to the current search, the search result rankings will change. The
user may see repeated results between the pages as user paginating. To ensure a good
user experience, we should reuse the same `IndexSearcher` within a search session so
while user paginating, it will always be searched against the same `IndexSearcher`. This
is where `SearcherLifetimeManager` can help. `SearcherLifetimeManager` is used
to hold on to an `IndexSearcher` and return an identifying token. As the user paginates
through the result, we can use the token to retrieve `IndexSearcher` to continue with the
search without worrying about an index refresh affecting the current search session. When
the user finishes with the search, the `IndexSearcher` can simply be returned back to
`SearcherLifetimeManager`.

As we continue to maintain `IndexSearcher` for each search session, it is inevitable that the number of `IndexSearchers` will increase overtime. To clean up the old `IndexSearchers` that are no longer in use, we can use the `SearcherLifetimeManager`'s prune method to perform the sweep. We will need to make sure `IndexSearcher` is released, by calling the `release` method after every use, so that `SearcherLifetimeManager` knows which ones can be dropped. When calling the `prune` method, we can specify a `PruneByAge` value to drop `IndexSearchers` that are older by a certain age.

The following diagram depicts the main actions of `SearcherLifetimeManager`:

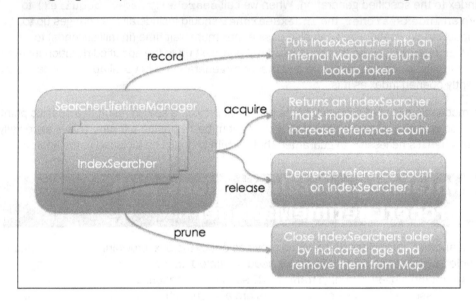

How to do it...

Here is the sample code on `SearcherLifetimeManager`:

```
DirectoryReader directoryReader = DirectoryReader.open(indexWriter,
true);
IndexSearcher indexSearcher = new IndexSearcher(directoryReader);

SearcherLifetimeManager searcherLifetimeManager = new
SearcherLifetimeManager();
long searcherToken = searcherLifetimeManager.record(indexSearcher);

indexSearcher = searcherLifetimeManager.acquire(searcherToken);
```

```
if (indexSearcher != null) {
    try {
        // perform search here
    } finally {
        searcherLifetimeManager.release(indexSearcher);
        indexSearcher = null;
    }
} else {
    // searcher was pruned, notify user that search session has
timed out
}

searcherLifetimeManager.prune(new
SearcherLifetimeManager.PruneByAge(600.0));
```

How it works...

Here, we first open an `IndexSearcher` with an `IndexWriter`. Then, we instantiate a `SearcherLifetimeManager` and call its record method to hold on to the current `IndexSearcher`. The returning long value is a token we will use to recall this `IndexSearcher` by calling the acquire method. Then, we perform a search and release the `IndexSearcher`. Also, lastly, we call prune to remove any `IndexSearcher` that's older than 600 seconds.

Performance tuning: latency and throughput

Search latency is the measure of time between the start of a query and the delivery of a search result. Throughput is the number of actions the system can sustain in a given time period. Ideally, we want latency to be one second or less and throughput, obviously, to be as high as possible. Both of these measurements are important factors in determining your hardware needs and infrastructure design.

Latency and throughput are correlated; both depend heavily on the available system resources, for example, CPU, IO, memory, and so on. In a single instance, lower latency will naturally increase throughput. When lowering latency is not attainable, we will have to resort to add more hardware to boost the number of instances to serve concurrently. Hardware sizing, at this point, will be a simple math of the desired throughput divided by a single instance's throughput to determine the number of servers that are needed for the search.

How to do it...

There are a several things to consider when performance tuning a Lucene search application. Let's review what can be done on the hardware side, which should bring us some immediate benefits to improve latency. Here are some items to consider:

▸ Use a solid-state disk for index storage. This will improve the load time and index update time.

▸ Put as much RAM as possible to your system. The ideal set up is to fit the entire index in memory. That'll reduce latency in the index lookup compared to a **hard disk drive** (**HDD**). Accessing data in RAM is a thousand times faster than using HDD. We can eliminate slow IO lookup when we access everything in memory. This will bring the most gain compared to other upgrades.

▸ Get as many CPU cores as possible as this will improve throughput by allowing more threads to run concurrently. This is also assuming that each CPU core is fast enough to deliver results in less than a second.

Aside from hardware upgrades, there are also techniques we can leverage in configuration and architecture to help improve performance. Let's look at some of these techniques:

▸ Use `NRTCachingDirectory` to wrap around a Directory, to keep all the uncommitted changes in memory for a NRT search. This will bring an immediate improvement in latency, as all the outstanding updates can be retrieved from RAM.

▸ Minimize the reopening of `IndexWriter` and `IndexSearcher`. Maintain a single `IndexSearcher` for as long as possible to avoid additional memory consumption in maintaining multiple `IndexSearchers`. However, in a NRT implementation, it's inevitable to have frequent refreshes. We should use a separate thread to trigger the refresh in the background, while keeping an existing opened `IndexSearcher` serving searches until the fresh index is warmed up. This approach will maintain the same level of latency between refreshes.

▸ Profile the JVM to find out if garbage collection kicked off too frequently as that indicates that there is insufficient memory. Maximize the amount of memory that can be allocated to JVM: if we can allocate more than 2 GB of RAM, use a 64-bit JVM so that we can map more memory.

▸ Multithread the application, which will increase throughput as we will be able to handle many requests at once.

▸ Warm up `FieldCache` when the index is refreshed before using it, so that the initial queries are not penalized by a slow response due to caches not being warmed up.

▸ Use `SearcherManager` to share `IndexSearcher` among many threads and minimize the number of opened `IndexSearchers`.

▸ Perform all index maintenance, for example,. merging segments in the background.

How it works...

It's easy to understand that more RAM equates to better performance, but how does Lucene treat memory management behind the scenes? When we talk about warming up a reader, it's comprised of a number of things being moved into RAM such as `FieldCache`, norms, and index segments. These items are loaded lazily so it's important to have a warm up routine; usually, a number of queries that would hit all the areas of the index, in order to allow Lucene to load these items into cache. Once a reader is warmed up, it can then be released to the users. Lucene also relies on the OS's IO caching scheme to cache physical index files, so that the frequently accessed segments can benefit from OS caching. It's advisable that a memory swap should be turned off at the OS level to minimize OS from unloading any less frequently used `FieldCache` to disk. Swapping will potentially slow the search down to a crawl, as the disk IO is a lot slower than RAM access.

In NRT, when a reader is opened, any recent updates actually get flushed into a new segment and a new reader is opened including this new segment. More available RAM, in this case, will benefit NRT in speedily opening a reader.

The goal of all these techniques is to reduce latency and increase throughput. As mentioned earlier, sizing for hardware can be a simple math to determine a single instance throughput and use that as a guide to find out how much hardware we need, in order to attain the desired performance. Reducing latency is usually the first thing to consider when performance tuning because that will immediately impact throughput. When a latency tuning option is exhausted, we can look into tuning throughput. We mentioned a few techniques to help increase throughput, but ideally we should focus on software tuning first before looking into increasing hardware. That's because there may still be a room for improvement in a single server. For example, by increasing a number of threads, throughput will naturally increase as long as we have enough CPU cores to support concurrent access. Also, by increasing the JVM heap size and increasing caching in the application, we encourage more data lookup in the memory, which will certainly help to improve both latency and throughput.

6
Querying and Filtering Data

In this chapter, we will cover the following recipes:

- ▶ Performing advanced filtering
- ▶ Creating a custom filter
- ▶ Searching with QueryParser
- ▶ TermQuery and TermRangeQuery
- ▶ BooleanQuery
- ▶ PrefixQuery and WildcardQuery
- ▶ PhraseQuery and MultiPhraseQuery
- ▶ FuzzyQuery
- ▶ NumericRangeQuery
- ▶ DisjunctionMaxQuery
- ▶ RegexpQuery
- ▶ SpanQuery
- ▶ CustomScoreQuery

Introduction

When it comes to search application, usability is always a key element that either makes or breaks user impression. Lucene does an excellent job of giving you the essential tools to build and search an index. In this chapter, we will look into some more advanced techniques to query and filter data. We will arm you with more knowledge to put into your toolbox so that you can leverage your Lucene knowledge to build a user-friendly search application.

Performing advanced filtering

Before we start, let us try to revisit these questions: what is a filter and what is it for? In simple terms, a filter is used to narrow the search space or, in another words, search within a search. Filter and Query may seem to provide the same functionality, but there is a significant difference between the two. Scores are calculated in querying to rank results, based on their relevancy to the search terms, while a filter has no effect on scores. It's not uncommon that users may prefer to navigate through a hierarchy of filters in order to land on the relevant results. You may often find yourselves in a situation where it is necessary to refine a result set so that users can continue to search or navigate within a subset. With the ability to apply filters, we can easily provide such search refinements. Another situation is data security where some parts of the data in the index are protected. You may need to include an additional filter behind the scene that's based on user access level so that users are restricted to only seeing items that they are permitted to access. In both of these contexts, Lucene's filtering features will provide the capability to achieve the objectives.

Lucene has a few built-in filters that are designed to fit most of the real-world applications. If you do find yourself in a position where none of the built-in filters are suitable for the job, you can rest assured that Lucene's expansibility will allow you to build your own custom filters. Let us take a look at Lucene's built-in filters:

- **TermRangeFilter**: This is a filter that restricts results to a range of terms that are defined by lower bound and upper bound of a submitted range. This filter is best used on a single-valued field because on a tokenized field, any tokens within a range will return by this filter. This is for textual data only.

- **NumericRangeFilter**: Similar to `TermRangeFilter`, this filter restricts results to a range of numeric values.

- **FieldCacheRangeFilter**: This filter runs on top of the number of range filters, including `TermRangeFilter` and `NumericRangeFilter`. It caches filtered results using `FieldCache` for improved performance. FieldCache is stored in the memory, so performance boost can be upward of 100x faster than the normal range filter. Because it uses `FieldCache`, it's best to use this on a single-valued field only. This filter will not be applicable for multivalued field and when the available memory is limited, since it maintains `FieldCache` (in memory) on filtered results.

- **QueryWrapperFilter**: This filter acts as a wrapper around a Query object. This filter is useful when you have complex business rules that are already defined in a Query and would like to reuse for other business purposes. It constructs a Query to act like a filter so that it can be applied to other Queries. Because this is a filter, scoring results from the Query within is irrelevant.

- **PrefixFilter**: This filter restricts results that match what's defined in the prefix. This is similar to a substring match, but limited to matching results with a leading substring only.

- **FieldCacheTermsFilter**: This is a term filter that uses `FieldCache` to store the calculated results in memory. This filter works on a single-valued field only. One use of it is when you have a category field where results are usually shown by categories in different pages. The filter can be used as a demarcation by categories.

- **FieldValueFilter**: This filter returns a document containing one or more values on the specified field. This is useful as a preliminary filter to ensure that certain fields exist before querying.

- **CachingWrapperFilter**: This is a wrapper that adds a caching layer to a filter to boost performance. Note that this filter provides a general caching layer; it should be applied on a filter that produces a reasonably small result set, such as an exact match. Otherwise, larger results may unnecessarily drain the system's resources and can actually introduce performance issues.

If none of the above filters fulfill your business requirements, you can build your own, extending the Filter class and implementing its abstract method `getDocIdSet` (`AtomicReaderContext, Bits`).

How to do it...

Let's set up our test case with the following code:

```
Analyzer analyzer = new StandardAnalyzer();
Directory directory = new RAMDirectory();
IndexWriterConfig config = new
  IndexWriterConfig(Version.LATEST, analyzer);
IndexWriter indexWriter = new IndexWriter(directory, config);
  Document doc = new Document();
StringField stringField = new StringField("name", "",
  Field.Store.YES);
TextField textField = new TextField("content", "",
  Field.Store.YES);
IntField intField = new IntField("num", 0, Field.Store.YES);
doc.removeField("name"); doc.removeField("content");
doc.removeField("num");
```

```
stringField.setStringValue("First");
textField.setStringValue("Humpty Dumpty sat on a wall,");
intField.setIntValue(100);
doc.add(stringField); doc.add(textField); doc.add(intField);
indexWriter.addDocument(doc);
doc.removeField("name"); doc.removeField("content");
doc.removeField("num");
stringField.setStringValue("Second");
textField.setStringValue("Humpty Dumpty had a great fall.");
intField.setIntValue(200);
doc.add(stringField); doc.add(textField); doc.add(intField);
indexWriter.addDocument(doc);
doc.removeField("name"); doc.removeField("content");
doc.removeField("num");
stringField.setStringValue("Third");
textField.setStringValue("All the king's horses and all the king's
men");
intField.setIntValue(300);
doc.add(stringField); doc.add(textField); doc.add(intField);
indexWriter.addDocument(doc);
doc.removeField("name"); doc.removeField("content");
doc.removeField("num");
stringField.setStringValue("Fourth");
textField.setStringValue("Couldn't put Humpty together
  again.");
intField.setIntValue(400);
doc.add(stringField); doc.add(textField); doc.add(intField);
indexWriter.addDocument(doc);
indexWriter.commit();
indexWriter.close();
IndexReader indexReader = DirectoryReader.open(directory);
IndexSearcher indexSearcher = new IndexSearcher(indexReader);
```

How it works...

The preceding code adds four documents into an index. The four documents are:

- Document 1

  Name: First

  Content: Humpty Dumpty sat on a wall,

  Num: 100

- ▸ Document 2

  Name: Second

  Content: Humpty Dumpty had a great fall.

  Num: 200

- ▸ Document 3

  Name: Third

  Content: All the king's horses and all the king's men

  Num: 300

- ▸ Document 4

  Name: Fourth

  Content: Couldn't put Humpty together again.

  Num: 400

Here is our standard test case:

```
IndexReader indexReader = DirectoryReader.open(directory);
IndexSearcher indexSearcher = new IndexSearcher(indexReader);
Query query = new TermQuery(new Term("content", "humpty"));
TopDocs topDocs = indexSearcher.search(query, FILTER, 100);
System.out.println("Searching 'humpty'");
for (ScoreDoc scoreDoc : topDocs.scoreDocs) {
    doc = indexReader.document(scoreDoc.doc);
    System.out.println("name: " +
        doc.getField("name").stringValue() +
        " - content: " +
        doc.getField("content").stringValue() +
        " - num: " +
        doc.getField("num").stringValue());
}
indexReader.close();
```

Running the code as it is will produce the following output, assuming the FILTER variable is declared:

```
Searching 'humpty'
name: First - content: Humpty Dumpty sat on a wall, - num: 100
name: Second - content: Humpty Dumpty had a great fall. - num: 200
name: Fourth - content: Couldn't put Humpty together again. - num:
400
```

This is a simple search on the word `humpty`. The search would return the first, second, and fourth sentences.

Now, let's take a look at a `TermRangeFilter` example:

```
TermRangeFilter termRangeFilter =
TermRangeFilter.newStringRange("name", "A", "G", true, true);
```

Applying this filter to preceding search (by setting FILTER as `termRangeFilter`) will produce the following output:

```
Searching 'humpty'
name: First - content: Humpty Dumpty sat on a wall, - num: 100
name: Fourth - content: Couldn't put Humpty together again. - num:
400
```

Note that the second sentence is missing from the results due to this filter. This filter removes documents with `name` outside of `A` through `G`. Both first and fourth sentences start with `F` that's within the range so their results are included. The second sentence's name value `Second` is outside the range, so the document is not considered by the query.

Let's move on to `NumericRangeFilter`:

```
NumericRangeFilter numericRangeFilter =
NumericRangeFilter.newIntRange("num", 200, 400, true, true);
```

This filter will produce the following results:

```
Searching 'humpty'
name: Second - content: Humpty Dumpty had a great fall. - num: 200
name: Fourth - content: Couldn't put Humpty together again. - num:
400
```

Note that the first sentence is missing from results. It's because its num `100` is outside the specified numeric range 200 to 400 in `NumericRangeFilter`.

Next one is `FieldCacheRangeFilter`:

```
FieldCacheRangeFilter fieldCacheTermRangeFilter =
FieldCacheRangeFilter.newStringRange("name", "A", "G", true, true);
```

The output of this filter is similar to the `TermRangeFilter` example:

```
Searching 'humpty'
name: First - content: Humpty Dumpty sat on a wall, - num: 100
name: Fourth - content: Couldn't put Humpty together again. - num: 400
```

This filter provides a caching layer on top of `TermRangeFilter`. Results are similar, but performance is a lot better because the calculated results are cached in memory for the next retrieval.

Next is `QueryWrapperFiler`:

```
QueryWrapperFilter queryWrapperFilter = new QueryWrapperFilter(new
TermQuery(new Term("content", "together")));
```

This example will produce this result:

```
Searching 'humpty'
name: Fourth - content: Couldn't put Humpty together again. - num:
400
```

This filter wraps around `TermQuery` on term `together` on the `content` field. Since the fourth sentence is the only one that contains the word "together" search results is limited to this sentence only.

Next one is `PrefixFilter`:

```
PrefixFilter prefixFilter = new PrefixFilter(new Term("name",
"F"));
```

This filter produces the following:

```
Searching 'humpty'
name: First - content: Humpty Dumpty sat on a wall, - num: 100
name: Fourth - content: Couldn't put Humpty together again. - num:
400
```

This filter limits results where the `name` field begins with letter *F*. In this case, the first and fourth sentences both have the `name` field that begins with *F* (*First* and *Fourth*); hence, the results.

Next is `FieldCacheTermsFilter`:

```
FieldCacheTermsFilter fieldCacheTermsFilter = new
FieldCacheTermsFilter("name", "First");
```

This filter produces the following:

```
Searching 'humpty'
name: First - content: Humpty Dumpty sat on a wall, - num: 100
```

This filter limits results with the name containing the word first. Since the first sentence is the only one that contains first, only one sentence is returned in search results.

Next is `FieldValueFilter`:

```
FieldValueFilter fieldValueFilter = new FieldValueFilter("name1");
```

This would produce the following:

```
Searching 'humpty'
```

Note that there are no results because this filter limits results in which there is at least one value on the filed `name1`. Since the `name1` field doesn't exist in our current example, no documents are returned by this filter; hence, zero results.

Next is `CachingWrapperFilter`:

```
TermRangeFilter termRangeFilter = TermRangeFilter.
newStringRange("name", "A", "G", true, true);
CachingWrapperFilter cachingWrapperFilter = new CachingWrapperFilter(t
ermRangeFilter);
```

This wrapper wraps around the same `TermRangeFilter` from above, so the result produced is similar:

```
Searching 'humpty'
name: First - content: Humpty Dumpty sat on a wall, - num: 100
name: Fourth - content: Couldn't put Humpty together again. - num:
400
```

Filters work in conjunction with Queries to refine the search results. As you may have already noticed, the benefit of Filter is its ability to cache results, while Query calculates in real time. When choosing between Filter and Query, you will want to ask yourself whether the search (or filtering) will be repeated. Provided you have enough memory allocation, a cached Filter will always provide a positive impact to search experiences.

Creating a custom filter

Now that we've seen numerous examples on Lucene's built-in Filters, we are ready for a more advanced topic, custom filters. There are a few important components we need to go over before we start: `FieldCache`, `SortedDocValues`, and `DocIdSet`. We will be using these items in our example to help you gain practical knowledge on the subject.

In the `FieldCache`, as you already learned, is a cache that stores field values in memory in an array structure. It's a very simple data structure as the slots in the array basically correspond to DocIds. This is also the reason why `FieldCache` only works for a single-valued field. A slot in an array can only hold a single value. Since this is just an array, the lookup time is constant and very fast.

The `SortedDocValues` has two internal data mappings for values' lookup: a dictionary mapping an ordinal value to a field value and a DocId to an ordinal value (for the field value) mapping. In the dictionary data structure, the values are deduplicated, dereferenced, and sorted. There are two methods of interest in this class: `getOrd(int)` and `lookupTerm(BytesRef)`. The `getOrd(int)` returns an ordinal for a `DocId (int)` and `lookupTerm(BytesRef)` returns an ordinal for a field value. This data structure is the opposite of the inverted index structure, as this provides a DocId to value lookup (similar to `FieldCache`), instead of value to a DocId lookup.

DocIdSet, as the name implies, is a set of DocId. A `FieldCacheDocIdSet` subclass we will be using is a combination of this set and `FieldCache`. It iterates through the set and calls `matchDoc(int)` to find all the matching documents to be returned.

In our example, we will be building a simple user security Filter to determine which documents are eligible to be viewed by a user based on the user ID and group ID. The group ID is assumed to be hereditary, where as a smaller ID inherits rights from a larger ID. For example, the following will be our group ID model in our implementation:

```
10 - admin
20 - manager
30 - user
40 - guest
```

A user with group ID 10 will be able to access documents where its group ID is 10 or above.

How to do it...

Here is our custom Filter, `UserSecurityFilter`:

```
public class UserSecurityFilter extends Filter {

  private String userIdField;
  private String groupIdField;
  private String userId;
  private String groupId;

  public UserSecurityFilter(String userIdField, String
    groupIdField, String userId, String groupId) {
    this.userIdField = userIdField;
    this.groupIdField = groupIdField;
    this.userId = userId;
    this.groupId = groupId;
  }
```

```
public DocIdSet getDocIdSet(AtomicReaderContext context, Bits
  acceptDocs) throws IOException {
  final SortedDocValues userIdDocValues =
  FieldCache.DEFAULT.getTermsIndex(context.reader(),
  userIdField);
  final SortedDocValues groupIdDocValues =
  FieldCache.DEFAULT.getTermsIndex(context.reader(),
    groupIdField);

  final int userIdOrd = userIdDocValues.lookupTerm(new
    BytesRef(userId));
  final int groupIdOrd = groupIdDocValues.lookupTerm(new
    BytesRef(groupId));

  return new FieldCacheDocIdSet(context.reader().maxDoc(),
  acceptDocs) {
    @Override
    protected final boolean matchDoc(int doc) {
      final int userIdDocOrd = userIdDocValues.getOrd(doc);
      final int groupIdDocOrd = groupIdDocValues.getOrd(doc);
      return userIdDocOrd == userIdOrd || groupIdDocOrd >=
        groupIdOrd;
    }
  };
  }
}
```

This Filter accepts four arguments in its constructor:

  ▶ userIdField: This is the field name for user ID
  ▶ groupIdField: This is the field name for group ID
  ▶ userId: This is the current session's user ID
  ▶ groupId: This is the current session's group ID of the user

Then, we implement getDocIdSet(AtomicReaderContext, Bits) to perform our filtering by userId and groupId. We first acquire two SortedDocValues, one for the user ID and one for the group ID, based on the Field names we obtained from the constructor. Then, we look up the ordinal values for the current session's user ID and group ID. The return value is a new FieldCacheDocIdSet object implementing its matchDoc(int) method. This is where we compare both the user ID and group ID to determine whether a document is viewable by the user. A match is true when the user ID matches and the document's group ID is greater than or equal to the user's group ID.

To test this Filter, we will set up our index as follows:

```
Analyzer analyzer = new StandardAnalyzer();
Directory directory = new RAMDirectory();
IndexWriterConfig config = new
  IndexWriterConfig(Version.LATEST, analyzer);
IndexWriter indexWriter = new IndexWriter(directory, config);
Document doc = new Document();
StringField stringFieldFile = new StringField("file", "",
  Field.Store.YES);
StringField stringFieldUserId = new StringField("userId", "",
  Field.Store.YES);
StringField stringFieldGroupId = new StringField("groupId",
  "", Field.Store.YES);

doc.removeField("file"); doc.removeField("userId");
  doc.removeField("groupId");
stringFieldFile.setStringValue("Z:\\shared\\finance\\2014-
  sales.xls");
stringFieldUserId.setStringValue("1001");
stringFieldGroupId.setStringValue("20");
doc.add(stringFieldFile); doc.add(stringFieldUserId);
  doc.add(stringFieldGroupId);
indexWriter.addDocument(doc);

doc.removeField("file"); doc.removeField("userId");
  doc.removeField("groupId");
stringFieldFile.setStringValue("Z:\\shared\\company\\2014-
  policy.doc");
stringFieldUserId.setStringValue("1101");
stringFieldGroupId.setStringValue("30");
doc.add(stringFieldFile); doc.add(stringFieldUserId);
doc.add(stringFieldGroupId);
indexWriter.addDocument(doc);
doc.removeField("file"); doc.removeField("userId");
doc.removeField("groupId");
stringFieldFile.setStringValue("Z:\\shared\\company\\2014-
terms-and-conditions.doc");
stringFieldUserId.setStringValue("1205");
stringFieldGroupId.setStringValue("40");
doc.add(stringFieldFile); doc.add(stringFieldUserId);
doc.add(stringFieldGroupId);
indexWriter.addDocument(doc);
indexWriter.commit();
indexWriter.close();
```

The setup adds three documents to our index with different user IDs and group ID settings in each document, as follows:

```
UserSecurityFilter userSecurityFilter = new
  UserSecurityFilter("userId", "groupId", "1001", "40");
IndexReader indexReader = DirectoryReader.open(directory);
IndexSearcher indexSearcher = new IndexSearcher(indexReader);
Query query = new MatchAllDocsQuery();
TopDocs topDocs = indexSearcher.search(query, userSecurityFilter,
  100);
for (ScoreDoc scoreDoc : topDocs.scoreDocs) {
  doc = indexReader.document(scoreDoc.doc);
  System.out.println("file: " +
    doc.getField("file").stringValue() +" - userId: " +
      doc.getField("userId").stringValue() + " - groupId: " +
        doc.getField("groupId").stringValue());
}
indexReader.close();
```

We initialize `UserSecurityFilter` with the matching names for user ID and group ID fields, and set it up with user ID `1001` and group ID `40`. For our test and search, we use `MatchAllDocsQuery` to basically search without any queries (as it will return all the documents). Here is the output from the code:

```
file: Z:\shared\finance\2014-sales.xls - userId: 1001 - groupId:
20
file: Z:\shared\company\2014-terms-and-conditions.doc - userId:
1205 - groupId: 40
```

The search specifically filters by user ID `1001`, so the first document is returned because its user ID is also `1001`. The third document is returned because its group ID, `40`, is greater than or equal to the user's group ID, which is also `40`.

Searching with QueryParser

QueryParser is an interpreter tool that transforms a search string into a series of Query clauses. It's not absolutely necessary to use QueryParser to perform a search, but it's a great feature that empowers users by allowing the use of search modifiers. A user can specify a phrase match by putting quotes (") around a phrase. A user can also control whether a certain term or phrase is required by putting a plus ("+") sign in front of the term or phrase, or use a minus ("-") sign to indicate that the term or phrase must not exist in results. For Boolean searches, the user can use AND and OR to control whether all terms or phrases are required.

To do a field-specific search, you can use a colon (":") to specify a field for a search (for example, content:humpty would search for the term "humpty" in the field "content"). For wildcard searches, you can use the standard wildcard character asterisk ("*") to match 0 or more characters, or a question mark ("?") for matching a single character. As you can see, the general syntax for a search query is not complicated, though the more advanced modifiers can seem daunting to new users. In this section, we will cover more advanced QueryParser features to show you what you can do to customize a search.

How to do it..

Let's look at the options that we can set in QueryParser. The following is a piece of code snippet for our setup:

```
Analyzer analyzer = new StandardAnalyzer();
Directory directory = new RAMDirectory();
IndexWriterConfig config = new IndexWriterConfig(Version.LATEST,
analyzer);
IndexWriter indexWriter = new IndexWriter(directory, config);
Document doc = new Document();
StringField stringField = new StringField("name", "", Field.Store.
YES);
TextField textField = new TextField("content", "", Field.Store.YES);
IntField intField = new IntField("num", 0, Field.Store.YES);

doc.removeField("name"); doc.removeField("content"); doc.
removeField("num");
stringField.setStringValue("First");
textField.setStringValue("Humpty Dumpty sat on a wall,");
intField.setIntValue(100);
doc.add(stringField); doc.add(textField); doc.add(intField);
indexWriter.addDocument(doc);

doc.removeField("name"); doc.removeField("content"); doc.
removeField("num");
stringField.setStringValue("Second");
textField.setStringValue("Humpty Dumpty had a great fall.");
intField.setIntValue(200);
doc.add(stringField); doc.add(textField); doc.add(intField);
indexWriter.addDocument(doc);
```

```
doc.removeField("name"); doc.removeField("content"); doc.
removeField("num");
stringField.setStringValue("Third");
textField.setStringValue("All the king's horses and all the king's
men");
intField.setIntValue(300);
doc.add(stringField); doc.add(textField); doc.add(intField);
indexWriter.addDocument(doc);

doc.removeField("name"); doc.removeField("content"); doc.
removeField("num");
stringField.setStringValue("Fourth");
textField.setStringValue("Couldn't put Humpty together again.");
intField.setIntValue(400);
doc.add(stringField); doc.add(textField); doc.add(intField);
indexWriter.addDocument(doc);

indexWriter.commit();
indexWriter.close();

IndexReader indexReader = DirectoryReader.open(directory);
IndexSearcher indexSearcher = new IndexSearcher(indexReader);
QueryParser queryParser = new QueryParser("content", analyzer);
// configure queryParser here
Query query = queryParser.parse("humpty");
TopDocs topDocs = indexSearcher.search(query, 100);
```

We add four documents and instantiate a `QueryParser` object with a default field and an analyzer. We will be using the same analyzer that was used in indexing to ensure that we apply the same text treatment to maximize matching capability.

Wildcard search

The query syntax for a wildcard search is the asterisk ("`*`") or question mark ("`?`") character. Here is a sample query:

```
Query query = queryParser.parse("humpty*");
```

This query will return the first, second, and fourth sentences. By default, QueryParser does not allow a leading wildcard character because it has a significant performance impact. A leading wildcard would trigger a full scan on the index since any term can be a potential match. In essence, even an inverted index would become rather useless for a leading wildcard character search. However, it's possible to override this default setting to allow a leading wildcard character by calling `setAllowLeadingWildcard(true)`. You can go ahead and run this example with different search strings to see how this feature works.

Depending on where the wildcard character(s) is placed, QueryParser will produce either a `PrefixQuery` or `WildcardQuery`. In this specific example in which there is only one wildcard character and it's not the leading character, a `PrefixQuery` will be produced.

Term range search

We can produce a `TermRangeQuery` by using `TO` in a search string. The range has the following syntax:

```
[start TO end]   - inclusive
{start TO end} - exclusive
```

As indicated, the angle brackets *([and])* is inclusive of start and end terms, and curly brackets *({ and })* is exclusive of start and end terms. It's also possible to mix these brackets to inclusive on one side and exclusive on the other side.

Here is a code snippet:

```
Query query = queryParser.parse("[aa TO c]");
```

This search will return the third and fourth sentences, as their beginning words are All and Couldn't, which are within the range. You can optionally analyze the range terms with the same analyzer by setting `setAnalyzeRangeTerms(true)`.

Autogenerated phrase query

QueryParser can automatically generate a `PhraseQuery` when there is more than one term in a search string. Here is a code snippet:

```
queryParser.setAutoGeneratePhraseQueries(true);
Query query = queryParser.parse("humpty+dumpty+sat");
```

This search will generate a PhraseQuery on the phrase *humpty dumpty sat* and will return the first sentence.

Date resolution

If you have a date field (by using `DateTools` to convert date to a string format) and would like to do a range search on date, it may be necessary to match the date resolution on a specific field. Here is a code snippet on setting the Date resolution:

```
queryParser.setDateResolution("date", DateTools.Resolution.DAY);
queryParser.setLocale(Locale.US);
queryParser.setTimeZone(TimeZone.getTimeZone("Am erica/New_York"));
```

This example sets the resolution to day granularity, locale to US, and time zone to New York. The locale and time zone settings are specific to the date format only.

Default operator

The default operator on a multiterm search string is OR. You can change the default to AND so all the terms are required. Here is a code snippet that will require all the terms in a search string:

```
queryParser.setDefaultOperator(QueryParser.Operator.AND);
Query query = queryParser.parse("humpty dumpty");
```

This example will return first and second sentences as these are the only two sentences with both *humpty* and *dumpty*.

Enable position increments

This setting is enabled by default. Its purpose is to maintain a position increment of the token that follows an omitted token, such as a token filtered by a StopFilter. This is useful in phrase queries when position increments may be important for scoring. Here is an example on how to enable this setting:

```
queryParser.setEnablePositionIncrements(true);
Query query = queryParser.parse("\"humpty dumpty\"");
```

In our scenario, it won't change our search results. This attribute only enables position increments information to be available in the resulting PhraseQuery.

Fuzzy query

Lucene's fuzzy search implementation is based on Levenshtein distance. It compares two strings and finds out the number of single character changes that are needed to transform one string to another. The resulting number indicates the closeness of the two strings. In a fuzzy search, a threshold number of edits is used to determine if the two strings are matched. To trigger a fuzzy match in QueryParser, you can use the tilde ~ character. There are a couple configurations in QueryParser to tune this type of query. Here is a code snippet:

```
queryParser.setFuzzyMinSim(2f);
queryParser.setFuzzyPrefixLength(3);
Query query = queryParser.parse("hump~");
```

This example will return first, second, and fourth sentences as the fuzzy match matches `hump` to `humpty` because these two words are missed by two characters. We tuned the fuzzy query to a minimum similarity to two in this example.

Lowercase expanded term

This configuration determines whether to automatically lowercase multiterm queries. An analyzer can do this already, so this is more like an overriding configuration that forces multiterm queries to be lowercased. Here is a code snippet:

```
queryParser.setLowercaseExpandedTerms(true);
Query query = queryParser.parse("\"Humpty Dumpty\"");
```

This code will lowercase our search string before search execution.

Phrase slop

Phrase search can be tuned to allow some flexibility in phrase matching. By default, phrase match is exact. Setting a slop value will give it some tolerance on terms that may not always be matched consecutively. Here is a code snippet that will demonstrate this feature:

```
queryParser.setPhraseSlop(3);
Query query = queryParser.parse("\"Humpty Dumpty wall\"");
```

Without setting a phrase slop, this phrase *Humpty Dumpty wall* will not have any matches. By setting phrase slop to three, it allows some tolerance so that this search will now return the first sentence. Go ahead and play around with this setting in order to get more familiarized with its behavior.

TermQuery and TermRangeQuery

A `TermQuery` is a very simple query that matches documents containing a specific term. The `TermRangeQuery` is, as its name implies, a term range with a lower and upper boundary for matching.

How to do it..

Here are a couple of examples on `TermQuery` and `TermRangeQuery`:

```
query = new TermQuery(new Term("content", "humpty"));
query = new TermRangeQuery("content", new BytesRef("a"), new
BytesRef("c"), true, true);
```

The first line is a simple query that matches the term `humpty` in the content field. The second line is a range query matching documents with the content that's sorted within *a* and *c*.

BooleanQuery

A BooleanQuery is a combination of other queries in which you can specify whether each subquery must, must not, or should match. These options provide the foundation to build up to logical operators of AND, OR, and NOT, which you can use in QueryParser. Here is a quick review on QueryParser syntax for BooleanQuery:

▸ "+" means required; for example, a search string +*humpty dumpty* equates to must match *humpty* and should match "dumpty"

▸ "-" means must not match; for example, a search string -`humpty dumpty` equates to must not match *humpty* and should match *dumpty*

▸ AND, OR, and NOT are pseudo Boolean operators. Under the hood, Lucene uses `BooleanClause.Occur` to model these operators. The options for occur are MUST, `MUST_NOT`, and `SHOULD`. In an AND query, both terms must match. In an OR query, both terms should match. Lastly, in a NOT query, the term `MUST_NOT` exists. For example, `humpty AND dumpty` means must match both humpty and dumpty, humpty *OR* dumpty means should match either or both humpty or dumpty, and *NOT* humpty means the term humpty must not exist in matching.

As mentioned, rudimentary clauses of BooleanQuery have three option: must match, must not match, and should match. These options allow us to programmatically create Boolean operations through an API.

How to do it..

Here is a code snippet that demonstrates `BooleanQuery`:

```
BooleanQuery query = new BooleanQuery();
query.add(new BooleanClause(
  new TermQuery(new Term("content", "humpty")),
  BooleanClause.Occur.MUST));
  query.add(new BooleanClause(new TermQuery(
  new Term("content", "dumpty")),
  BooleanClause.Occur.MUST));
  query.add(new BooleanClause(new TermQuery(
  new Term("content", "wall")),
  BooleanClause.Occur.SHOULD));
  query.add(new BooleanClause(new TermQuery(
  new Term("content", "sat")),
  BooleanClause.Occur.MUST_NOT));
```

How it works...

In this demonstration, we will use `TermQuery` to illustrate the building of `BooleanClauses`. It's equivalent to this logic: (`humpty AND dumpty`) OR wall NOT sat. This code will return the second sentence from our setup. Because of the last `MUST_NOT` BooleanClause on the word "sat", the first sentence is filtered from the results. Note that BooleanClause accepts two arguments: a Query and a `BooleanClause.Occur`. `BooleanClause.Occur` is where you specify the matching options: MUST, MUST_NOT, and SHOULD.

PrefixQuery and WildcardQuery

PrefixQuery, as the name implies, matches documents with terms starting with a specified prefix. WildcardQuery allows you to use wildcard characters for wildcard matching.

A PrefixQuery is somewhat similar to a WildcardQuery in which there is only one wildcard character at the end of a search string. When doing a wildcard search in QueryParser, it would return either a PrefixQuery or WildcardQuery, depending on the wildcard character's location. PrefixQuery is simpler and more efficient than WildcardQuery, so it's preferable to use PrefixQuery whenever possible. That's exactly what QueryParser does.

How to do it...

Here is a code snippet to demonstrate both Query types:

```
PrefixQuery query = new PrefixQuery(new Term("content", "hum"));
WildcardQuery query2 = new WildcardQuery(new Term("content",
"*um*"));
```

How it works...

Both queries would return the same results from our setup. The PrefixQuery will match anything that starts with `hum` and the WildcardQuery would match anything that contains `um`.

PhraseQuery and MultiPhraseQuery

A PhraseQuery matches a particular sequence of terms, while a MultiPhraseQuery gives you an option to match multiple terms in the same position. For example, MultiPhrasQuery supports a phrase such as humpty (dumpty *OR* together) in which it matches humpty in position *0* and dumpty or together in position *1*.

How to do it...

Here is a code snippet to demonstrate both Query types:

```
PhraseQuery query = new PhraseQuery();
query.add(new Term("content", "humpty"));
query.add(new Term("content", "together"));
MultiPhraseQuery query2 = new MultiPhraseQuery();
Term[] terms1 = new Term[1];
terms1[0] = new Term("content", "humpty");
Term[] terms2 = new Term[2];
terms2[0] = new Term("content", "dumpty");
terms2[1] = new Term("content", "together");
query2.add(terms1);
query2.add(terms2);
```

How it works...

The first Query, PhraseQuery, searches for the phrase humpty together. The second Query, MultiPhraseQuery, searches for the phrase humpty (dumpty OR together). The first Query would return sentence four from our setup, while the second Query would return sentence one, two, and four. Note that in MultiPhraseQuery, multiple terms in the same position are added as an array.

FuzzyQuery

A FuzzyQuery matches terms based on similarity, using the Damerau-Levenshtein algorithm. We are not going into the details of the algorithm as it is outside of our topic. What we need to know is a fuzzy match is measured in the number of edits between terms. FuzzyQuery allows a maximum of 2 edits. For example, between "humptX" and humpty is first edit and between humpXX and humpty are two edits. There is also a requirement that the number of edits must be less than the minimum term length (of either the input term or candidate term). As another example, *ab* and *abcd* would not match because the number of edits between the two terms is 2 and it's not greater than the length of *ab*, which is 2.

How to do it...

Here is a code snippet to demonstrate FuzzyQuery:

```
FuzzyQuery query = new FuzzyQuery(new Term("content", "humpXX"));
```

How it works...

This Query will return sentences one, two, and four from our setup, as humpXX matches humpty within the two edits. In QueryParser, FuzzyQuery can be triggered by the tilde (~) sign. An equivalent search string would be `humpXX~`.

NumericRangeQuery

NumericRangeQuery is similar to NumericRangeFilter, in which you can specify lower bound and upper bound values for matching. To ensure search quality, make sure the numeric type (`IntField`, `FloatField`, `LongField`, and `DoubleField`) matches between the search and indexed field.

How to do it...

Here is a code snippet to demonstrate `NumericRangeQuery`:

```
Query query = NumericRangeQuery.newIntRange("num", 0, 200, true,
true);
```

How it works...

This example will return sentence one and two from our setup. Note that we need to specify a numeric type (`newIntRange`) when creating a query. It accepts five parameters: name of the field, lower bound, upper bound, inclusive of a lower value, and inclusive of an upper value.

DisjunctionMaxQuery

This query type sounds a little funny and can be confusing at first. It's like a BooleanQuery that contains a number of subqueries. Instead of combining scores from each sub-Query, it returns the maximum score from one of the subqueries. The reason for this is that matching may match on multiple fields, and a match on more important fields (should have a higher score) can sometimes have an equivalent score with matching on less important fields due to the number of matching terms. For example, let's say we have a book store application, in which we have a book title and body in our index, and let's say we are searching for *The Old Man and the Sea*. A match on the title would return a very high score. However, it's possible that there may be another book with the similar title, but with more matching in the body—for example, *Young Man and the Sea*—that would return a higher combined (between the title and body) score.

In this case, a perfectly matched title may not be returned as a number one result. It may instead be returned as a second result, due to combined score strategy. This is where DisjunctionMaxQuery can help. As the name suggests, it's a disjunction of multiple Queries and only the one that returns the maximum score matters. In the situation in which there are ties between sub-Queries, you can use a tiebreaker multiplier to break the tie so that the term that matched in multiple fields may get judged better than the term matching in only one field.

According to Lucene's Javadoc (`http://lucene.apache.org/core/4_10_2/core/org/apache/lucene/search/DisjunctionMaxQuery.html`), the tiebreaker is described as:

The score of each nonmaximum disjunction for a document is multiplied by this weight and added into the final score. If nonzero, the value should be small, on the order of 0.1, which says that the 10 occurrences of the word in a lower-scored field that is also in a higher scored field is just as good as a unique word in the lower-scored field (that is, one that is not in any higher-scored field.

How to do it...

Here is a code snippet:

```
PhraseQuery phraseQuery = new PhraseQuery();
phraseQuery.add(new Term("content", "humpty"));
phraseQuery.add(new Term("content", "together"));

DisjunctionMaxQuery query = new DisjunctionMaxQuery(0.1f);
query.add(new TermQuery(new Term("name", "First")));
query.add(phraseQuery);
```

How it works...

In this example, we create a DisjunctionMaxQuery with two Queries. The first is a PhraseQuery with phrase `"humpty together"` and the second is a TermQuery against the `"name"` field with the term `"First"`. The tiebreaker multiplier is set to `0.1f`, but it's actually not applied in this test case because we don't have to break any ties. The results will bring back sentence four and then sentence one from our setup. This is because the match on PhraseQuery has a better score than a match in TermQuery.

RegexpQuery

Lucene also offers regular expression support in Query. Lucene's favor of RegExp is fast based on benchmark testing. However, it can be slow if the expression begins with `".*"`. For more information about Lucene's RegExp syntax, refer to `http://lucene.apache.org/core/4_10_2/core/org/apache/lucene/search/RegexpQuery.html`.

How to do it...

Here is a code snippet:

```
RegexpQuery query = new RegexpQuery(new Term("content", ".um.*"));
```

`RegexpQuery` accepts term as an argument where term would contain `Regexp`. In this test case, we try to match anything that contains the letter "um" with one leading character. The expression will return sentence one, two, and four from our setup.

SpanQuery

SpanQuery offers the ability to restrict matching by Term positions. It shines when you want to match multiple terms that are close to each other, but not exactly matched as a phrase. It's similar to PhraseQuery with a slop set greater than zero, but it gives you more options to control how matching is done. For instance, say we want to search for terms `"humpty"` and `"wall"` from our test setup so that we can match on the sentence `"Humpty Dumpty sat on a wall"`. We can perform this search using either PhraseQuery or SpanQuery with a slop set to 4; both Queries would match. So let's say we switch the two Terms around. Now, we have Terms in this order, `"wall"` and `"humpty"`. PhraseQuery will fail to find a match because the Terms are out of order. SpanQuery has an option to match, Terms out of order so that we can still find a match even when the Terms' order is reversed.

SpanQuery has other useful functionalities as well. We will explore each SpanQuery type in detail:

- `SpanTermQuery`: This acts as a base unit for other `SpanQuery`. If this is used as a stand-alone, it behaves just like `TermQuery`.

- `SpanNearQuery`: This match spans (for example, `SpanTermQuery`) near each other specified by a slop and whether the spans should be in order.

- `SpanFirstQuery`: This match spans near the beginning of the field within a specified end position. Say we are searching for the term `sat` and expect to match *Humpty Dumpty sat on a wall*, then the end position will have to be 3 or higher in order to meet the matching criteria as `sat` is on position `3`.

- `SpanNotQuery`: This Query accepts two parameters: an include `SpanQuery` and an exclude `SpanQuery`. A match is found when the include `SpanQuery` match does not overlap with the exclude `SpanQuery`. For example, the include `SpanQuery` is `"dumpty"` and `"wall"`. Running this Query alone will return `"Humpty Dumpty sat on a wall"`. Let's say the exclude `SpanQuery` is `"sat"`. This will negate the search because `"sat"` is within the include Query (between `"Dumpty"` and `"wall"`). Thus, the results will be empty.

- ▸ SpanOrQuery: This Query type is simple; it is just as the name implies. It returns matches when one of the SpanQueries is found.

- ▸ SpanMultiTermQueryWrapper: This is a wrapper class that wraps around any MultiTermQuery as a SpanQuery, so that it can be used within other SpanQuery classes.

- ▸ FieldMaskingSpanQuery: This wraps around a SpanQuery and masks the field value of the SpanQuery. The SpanQuery would still execute as normal (this wrapper does not modify the SpanQuery's matches). However, when you call getField(), it will return the field supplied to the constructor of the FieldMaskingSpanQuery.

- ▸ SpanPositionRangeQuery: This wraps around a SpanQuery and checks whether the match lies between a start and end position.

How to do it...

Let's take a look at some sample codes:

```
SpanNearQuery query1 = new SpanNearQuery(
    new SpanQuery[] {
        new SpanTermQuery(new Term("content", "wall")),
        new SpanTermQuery(new Term("content", "humpty")),
    },
    4,
    false);

SpanFirstQuery query2 = new SpanFirstQuery(
    new SpanTermQuery(new Term("content", "sat")),
    3
);

SpanNotQuery query3 = new SpanNotQuery(
    query1,
    new SpanTermQuery(new Term("content", "sat"))
);

SpanOrQuery query4 = new SpanOrQuery(
    query1,
    new SpanTermQuery(new Term("content", "together"))
);

WildcardQuery wildcard = new WildcardQuery(new Term("content",
"hum*"));
```

```
SpanQuery query5 = new SpanMultiTermQueryWrapper<WildcardQuery>(wildc
ard);

SpanQuery q1  = new SpanTermQuery(new Term("content", "dumpty"));
SpanQuery q2  = new SpanTermQuery(new Term("content2", "humpty"));
SpanQuery maskedQuery = new FieldMaskingSpanQuery(q2, "content");
Query query6 = new SpanNearQuery(new SpanQuery[]{q1, maskedQuery}, 4,
false);

SpanPositionRangeQuery query7 = new SpanPositionRangeQuery(
  new SpanTermQuery(new Term("content", "wall")), 5, 6);
```

How it works...

In `query1`, we set up a `SpanNearQuery` to search on two Terms—*wall* and *humpty*—with a maximum distance between the Terms set to 4, and the false parameter indicates that the Terms matching do not have to be in order. This search will match sentence one: "Humpty Dumpty sat on a wall". If distance is set to anything less than 4, we will not have a match because the distance between these two terms is exactly 4.

In `query2`, we have a `SpanFirstQuery` searching on the Term `"sat"`, and the end position is set to 3. This will match on the same sentence as well, because `"sat"` is on position 3. If the end position is less than 3, we will not have a match.

In `query3`, we have a `SpanNotQuery` with `query1` as include `SpanQuery` and Term `"sat"` as exclude query. This query will not return any matches because the exclude term `"sat"` is within `query1`'s span, between `"wall"` and `"humpty"`. Because there is an overlap between the two `SpanQuery`, the include `SpanQuery` match is filtered out.

In `query4`, we have a `SpanOrQuery` with a parameter `query1` and a Term `"together"`. This search will match on sentence one and four, where sentence four should be ranking first. It's because a multiterm match scores higher than a single term match. The search result is a union of each `SpanQuery`'s matches.

In `query5`, we demonstrate `SpanMultiTermQueryWrapper` by wrapping it around a `WildcardQuery` searching on the Term `"hum*"`. This search will bring back sentences one, two, and four as all these sentences contain the word `"Humpty"`, matched by the wildcard search `"hum*"`.

In `query6`, we can see how `FieldMaskingSpanQuery` masks a field for `SpanQuery q2`. This search will not find any matches. Note that `q2` is a `SpanTermQuery` on field *content2*, which doesn't exist. Even though we mask the field as *content* in `maskedQuery`, it doesn't change the fact that `q2` doesn't have a match. Because of this, the eventual `SpanNearQuery` will not have a match, either.

In `query7`, we demonstrate a `SpanPositionRangeQuery`, showing that the Term `"wall"` exists between positions 5 and 6. If you change the start and end positions to other values, it will not generate a match. This is a simple demonstration of how this Query is used.

CustomScoreQuery

When consideration of all the built-in features is exhausted and you still need more flexibility, it may be time to explore how to build a custom scoring mechanism to customize the search results ranking. Lucene has a `CustomScoreQuery` class that allows you to do just that. We can provide our own score provider by extending from this class, along with `CustomScoreProvider`. By extending `CustomScoreProvider`, we can override score calculation with our own implementation.

How to do it...

Let's take a look at how it's done. We will build a `CustomScoreQuery` that favors documents with terms that are anagrams of the querying Terms. For each anagram found, we increase the score by 1. The search results ranking will be augmented so that the documents with anagrammed Terms are ranked higher.

Here is the `AnagramQuery` class:

```
public class AnagramQuery extends CustomScoreQuery {
  private final String field;
  private final Set<String> terms = new HashSet<String>();
  public AnagramQuery(Query subquery, String field) {
    super(subquery);
    this.field = field;
    HashSet<Term> termSet = new HashSet<Term>();
    subquery.extractTerms(termSet);
    for (Term term : termSet) {
      terms.add(term.text());
    }
  }
  @Override
  protected CustomScoreProvider
    getCustomScoreProvider(AtomicReaderContext context) {
      return new AnagramQueryScoreProvider(context, field,
        terms);
  }
}
```

The class accepts a Query object and field name in the constructor. A set of querying Terms is extracted from the Query so that we can look for their anagrams in the field specified. Then, we override `getCustomScoreProvider` in order to return our own `AnagramQueryScoreProvider`, where we augment the score.

Here is the `AnagramQueryScoreProvider`:

```
public class AnagramQueryScoreProvider extends CustomScoreProvider {
  private String field;
  private Set<String> terms;
  public AnagramQueryScoreProvider(AtomicReaderContext
    context, String field, Set<String> terms) {
  super(context);
  this.field = field;
  this.terms = terms;
  }
  public float customScore(int doc, float subQueryScore,
    float valSrcScores[]) throws IOException {
  float score = subQueryScore;
  IndexReader indexReader = context.reader();
  Terms termsVector = indexReader.getTermVector(doc,
    field);
  if (termsVector == null) {
    return score;
  }
  TermsEnum termsEnum = termsVector.iterator(null);
  BytesRef term = null;
  String val = null;
  while ( (term = termsEnum.next()) != null ) {
  val = term.utf8ToString();
  if (terms.contains(val)) {
    continue;
  }
  for (String t : terms) {
    if (isAnagram(t, val)) {
      score += 1f;
      }
    }
  }
  return score;
  }
```

```
    private boolean isAnagram(String word1, String word2) {
    if (word1.length() != word2.length()) {
      return false;
    }
    char[] chars1 = word1.toCharArray();
    char[] chars2 = word2.toCharArray();
    Arrays.sort(chars1);
    Arrays.sort(chars2);
    return Arrays.equals(chars1, chars2);
    }
}
```

How it works...

The constructor accepts the current `AtomicReaderContext`, field name, and a set of term strings from `AnagramQuery`. The custom scoring happens in `customScore`. First, we retrieve the existing score from a sub-Query. Then, we retrieve `TermVector` on the supplied field name for the current document (`TermVector` should be enabled for the field during indexing). With `TermVector` on hand, we can iterate through all the terms in the document and compare with each querying terms to see if an anagram exists. For each anagram found, the score is increased by 1.

This is it. We can start using this `CustomScoreQuery` by wrapping it around another Query, such as `TermQuery`, in order to customize a search.

7
Flexible Scoring

We will take a deep dive into Lucene's scoring methodology and explore the available options in customization. Here is a list of topics we will cover in this chapter:

- Overriding similarity
- Implementing the BM25 model
- Implementing the language model
- Implementing the divergence from randomness model
- Implementing the information-based model

Introduction

Scoring is fundamental to Lucene's search capability and accuracy. Normally, you don't see scores in search results, but it's there to help sort results by relevancy. Knowing how scoring works, its boundary will help you make informed decisions in your application design.

The goal of scoring is to objectively calculate weights to rank already matched results. The contents that are more relevant to the search criteria are sorted before the less relevant ones. This is called relevancy ranking. Lucene employs a number of techniques to perform this calculation. The expandable nature of Lucene also allows you to customize scoring and expand from the default configuration. This flexibility is part of the appeal of Lucene's popularity. In this chapter, we will first look into Lucene's scoring methodology. Then, we will explore customization techniques to expand from default behavior. The intention of this chapter is to give you a primer into Lucene's scoring implementations. Hopefully, by the end of the chapter, you will gain a deeper understanding of Lucene's scoring technique and appreciate all the hard work that's been done by Lucene's developers.

To begin, let's try to understand how Lucene calculates a score at a high level. Lucene leverages both **Boolean model (BM)** and **vector space model (VSM)** of information retrieval internally. In Information Science, information retrieval is a field that deals with data querying. In this, there are several models of data representations. Boolean model and VSM are the two models Lucene uses to match and score results. The first part, Boolean Model, qualifies documents by matching a set of query terms to a set of indexed terms based on a Boolean expression derived from a query. Since Lucene's index is inverted with terms pointing at documents, Lucene can intersect document pointers to arrive at a result set of documents. In the second part, vector space model, Lucene models documents and queries as vectors where index terms are dimensions, and weights are the similarity between query terms and documents. The default similarity algorithm used is called **TFIDFSimilarity**. It calculates weight by comparing query terms to matched documents. The scores are then used to sort the result set.

Here is a more detailed explanation of each of TFIDFSimilarity's component. This is mainly for reference only and to show the fundamental concept of Lucene's scoring formula. It is be explained in layman's terms. Don't worry if the concept is still unclear at the end of this section as the actual implementation is already completed for you; you just need to know what the components are so you can build a custom scoring method on top of the existing formula. Although the whole concept is not simple, it's easier to digest if you take time to study one component at a time.

TFIDF (term frequency and inverse document frequency). Term frequency, as the name suggests, is the number of times a term appears in a document or query. Inverse document frequency is the inverse of TF where it represents the number of indexed documents containing a term. Building on top of this basic concept, here is a formula Lucene uses to score according to Lucene's documentation:

$$\text{score}(q,d) = \text{coord}(q,d) \ \text{queryNorm}(q) \sum_{t \text{ in } q} \left(\text{tf}(t \text{ in } d) \ \text{idf}(t) 2 \ t \ \text{getBoost}() \ \text{norm}(t,d) \right)$$

Note that this formula applies after matching; meaning documents are already found by a Query. Lucene scores each matched document individually using this formula. The formula is comprised of several components. We will explain each in detail:

  ▸ `tf(t in d)`: This is term's frequency in a given document. The higher the number of times a term appears, the higher the score. For `tf(t in q)`, term frequency in a query is always assumed to be 1. The default computation to score is:

$$\text{tf}(t \text{ in } d) = \text{frequency}^{1/2}$$

- `idf(t)`: This is inverse document frequency calculating a score based on inverse of docFreq, which is the number of documents in which the term t appears. The rarer the term, the higher the score that will be given. The default computation for this scoring is:

$$idf\left(t\right) = 1 + \log\left(\frac{numDocs}{docFreq + 1}\right)$$

- `coord(q,d)`: This determines a score based on the number of query terms that appear in a given document. A document that contains more query terms will receive a higher score.

- `queryNorm(q)`: This helps to normalize scores so that the scores between queries are comparable. It does not affect document rankings, as its purpose is to make a score from different queries that are comparable. The default formula is:

$$queryNorm\left(q\right) = queryNorm\left(sumOfSquaredWeights\right) = \frac{1}{sumOfSquaredWeights}$$

Note that `sumOfSquaredWeights` is determined by the Query's Weight Object.

- `t.getBoost()`: This returns a boost value at the search time for the term t in a Query, or returns a value that's set by the application calls to `setBoost()`.

- `norm(t,d)`: This calculates a partial score at indexing time with a couple of factors:

  - **Field boost**: This is a boost value that's set by calling `field.setBoost()` when adding a field to a document.

  - **lengthNorm**: This is computed based on the number of tokens in a Field. The shorter the Field, the higher the score.

- `computeNorm(FieldInvertState)`: This method combines these factors into a single score. The default computation is as follows:

$$norm\left(t,d\right) = lengthNorm \prod_{field\ f\ in\ d\ named\ as\ t} f\ boost()$$

Note that this score applies at indexing time only and cannot be altered at querying time.

Overriding similarity

The Similarity class is an abstract class that defines a set of components for score calculation. To steer away from default scoring, we can create a new class extending from the `DefaultSimilarity` (TFIDFSimilarity) or one of the other Similarity classes. We will perform some experimentation in this section to see how each scoring components affect the overall score.

Let's begin by reviewing Similarity's methods:

- ▶ `computeNorm(FieldInvertState)`: This calculates a normalization value for a Field at indexing time.

- ▶ `computeWeight(float, CollectionStatics, TermStatistics)`: This returns a `SimWeight` object to calculate a score. It accepts a boost (float) value for query-time boosting.

- ▶ `coord(int, int)`: This returns a score factor based on term overlap in a query. This value helps to integrate coordinate-level matching. The default is disabled with the returning value 1.

- ▶ `queryNorm(float)`: This generates a normalization value for a query. The value is also passed back to the Weight's normalize (float, float) method of each query term to make scores from different queries comparable.

- ▶ `simScorer(Similarity.SimWeight, AtomicReaderContext)`: This creates a new SimScorer object using SimWeight to score the matching documents in an index.

The Similarity class provides the basic framework in score calculation. In TFIDFSimilarity, some of these methods are declared final so we won't able to override them. For our experiment, we will extend from TFIDFSimilarity to see how we can influence scoring by overriding each scoring factor.

How to do it...

Let's start by extending from `DefaultSimilarity` (implements `TFIDFSimilarity`):

```
public class MySimilarity extends DefaultSimilarity {
    @Override
    public float coord(int overlap, int maxOverlap) {
        return super.coord(overlap, maxOverlap);
    }
    @Override
    public float idf(long docFreq, long numDocs) {
        return super.idf(docFreq, numDocs);
    }
```

```
    @Override
    public float lengthNorm(FieldInvertState state) {
        return super.lengthNorm(state);
    }
    @Override
    public float queryNorm(float sumOfSquaredWeights) {
        return super.queryNorm(sumOfSquaredWeights);
    }
    @Override
    public float scorePayload(int doc, int start, int end,
      BytesRef payload) {
        return super.scorePayload(doc, start, end, payload);
    }
    @Override
    public float sloppyFreq(int distance) {
        return super.sloppyFreq(distance);
    }
    @Override
    public float tf(float freq) {
        return super.tf(freq);
    }
}
```

Here is our test setup. We will be using `StandardAnalyzer`:

```
Analyzer analyzer = new StandardAnalyzer();
Directory directory = new RAMDirectory();
IndexWriterConfig config = new IndexWriterConfig(
    Version.LATEST, analyzer);
MySimilarity similarity = new MySimilarity();
config.setSimilarity(similarity);
IndexWriter indexWriter = new IndexWriter(directory, config);

Document doc = new Document();
TextField textField = new TextField("content", "", Field.Store.YES);

String[] contents = {"Humpty Dumpty sat on a wall,",
        "Humpty Dumpty had a great fall.",
        "All the king's horses and all the king's men",
        "Couldn't put Humpty together again."};
for (String content : contents) {
    textField.setStringValue(content);
    doc.removeField("content");
```

```
        doc.add(textField);
        indexWriter.addDocument(doc);
    }

    indexWriter.commit();

    IndexReader indexReader = DirectoryReader.open(directory);
    IndexSearcher indexSearcher = new IndexSearcher(indexReader);
    indexSearcher.setSimilarity(similarity);
    QueryParser queryParser = new QueryParser("content", analyzer);
    Query query = queryParser.parse("humpty dumpty");
    TopDocs topDocs = indexSearcher.search(query, 100);
    for (ScoreDoc scoreDoc : topDocs.scoreDocs) {
        doc = indexReader.document(scoreDoc.doc);
        System.out.println(scoreDoc.score + ": " +
          doc.getField("content").stringValue());
    }
```

How it works...

When you run the above code as it is, the results will appear as follows to search for the `humpty dumpty` string:

```
0.81518793: Humpty Dumpty sat on a wall,
0.7132894: Humpty Dumpty had a great fall.
0.13417153: Couldn't put Humpty together again.
```

The numeric value is the default scoring calculated by TFIDFSimilarity. Now, let's try to override each method and monitor how scoring and results change.

We will start with `coord(int, int)`. This method calculates a score factor by dividing the number of overlapping Query terms to documents by a maximum value. We will reverse this effect by boosting the score when there is only one matched term with the following code:

```
public float coord(int overlap, int maxOverlap) {
    if (overlap > 1) {
        return overlap / maxOverlap;
    } else {
        return 10;
    }
}
```

Here is the result of this override:

```
2.6834307: Couldn't put Humpty together again.
0.81518793: Humpty Dumpty sat on a wall,
0.7132894: Humpty Dumpty had a great fall.
```

Note that the order of the result changed because we put more weight on a single-term match than multiple terms.

Next, we will revert our previous changes to `coord(int, int)` and override the `idf(long, long)` method:

```
public float idf(long docFreq, long numDocs) {
    if (docFreq > 2) {
        return super.idf(docFreq, numDocs);
    } else {
        return super.idf(docFreq * 100, numDocs);
    }
}
```

We give a boost on match where `docFreq` is less than or equal to 2. Here is the result:

```
1.5418293: Humpty Dumpty sat on a wall,
1.3491007: Humpty Dumpty had a great fall.
0.07093847: Couldn't put Humpty together again.
```

We did not change the order of the results, but we introduced a bigger gap in scores when matched terms jump from 2 to higher numbers. Note that the first two records with two matching terms benefit from this alteration and the last record is penalized (by *docFreq * 100*). TDIDFSimilarity implemented this method with the formula: *log(numDocs/(docFreq+1)) + 1*.

Next, we will revert all changes and override the `lengthNorm(FieldInvertState)` method:

```
public float lengthNorm(FieldInvertState state) {
    if (state.getLength() % 2 == 1) {
        return super.lengthNorm(state) * 100;
    }
    return super.lengthNorm(state);
}
```

In this override, we favor Field value length in an odd number by boosting `lengthNorm` by a factor of 100. This change will produce the following results:

```
65.215034: Humpty Dumpty had a great fall.
12.267112: Couldn't put Humpty together again.
0.81518793: Humpty Dumpty sat on a wall,
```

Note that the second and third sentences benefit this change because their lengths are in odd numbers.

Next is `queryNorm(float)`. This method applies the score at a Query level so in our setup, a boost in this score will benefit all three results.

```
public float queryNorm(float sumOfSquaredWeights) {
    if (Math.round(sumOfSquaredWeights * 100f) % 2 == 0) {
        return super.queryNorm(sumOfSquaredWeights) * 100;
    }
    return super.queryNorm(sumOfSquaredWeights);
}
```

We favor the query when `sumOfSquaredWeights` hundredth decimal point is an even number when rounded up. This override will produce the following results:

```
81.51879: Humpty Dumpty sat on a wall,
71.32894: Humpty Dumpty had a great fall.
13.417152: Couldn't put Humpty together again.
```

To demonstrate `scorePayload`, we need to first customize an analyzer and a filter to add Payload to a term. Here is our `PayloadFilter`:

```
public class PayloadFilter extends TokenFilter {
    PayloadAttribute payloadAtt =
      addAttribute(PayloadAttribute.class);
    CharTermAttribute charTermAtt =
      addAttribute(CharTermAttribute.class);
    protected PayloadFilter(TokenStream input) {
      super(input);
    }
    public boolean incrementToken() throws IOException {
      if (!input.incrementToken()) { return false; }
    payloadAtt.setPayload(new BytesRef(
      PayloadHelper.encodeFloat(
        determinePayload(
          charTermAtt.toString())))));
    return true;
    }
```

```java
protected float determinePayload(String term) {
  float score = 1f;
  for (char c : term.toCharArray()) {
    switch (c) {
      case 'a':
        score += 0.1f;
      case 'e':
        score += 0.2f;
      case 'i':
        score += 0.4f;
      case 'o':
        score += 0.8f;
      case 'u':
        score += 1.6f;
      break;
    }
  }
  return score;
}
```

Also, here is our `PayloadAnalyzer`:

```java
public class PayloadAnalyzer extends StopwordAnalyzerBase {
    protected TokenStreamComponents createComponents(final String
      fieldName, final Reader reader) {
        final StandardTokenizer source = new
          StandardTokenizer(reader);
        TokenStream filter = new StandardFilter(source);
        filter = new LowerCaseFilter(filter);
        filter = new StopFilter(filter, stopwords);
        filter = new PayloadFilter(filter);
        return new TokenStreamComponents(source, filter);
    }
}
```

In this sample filter, we favor Term with vowel characters by issuing a float value as Payload. Next, we need to change our test setup by replacing Query with a BooleanQuery wrap around PayloadTermQuery to include Payload into score calculation:

```java
BooleanQuery query = new BooleanQuery();
query.add(new PayloadTermQuery(
  new Term("content", "humpty"),
  new AveragePayloadFunction(), true),
  BooleanClause.Occur.SHOULD);
```

```
query.add(new PayloadTermQuery(
new Term("content", "dumpty"),
new AveragePayloadFunction(), true),
BooleanClause.Occur.SHOULD);
```

This BooleanQuery is equivalent to an OR operation between the two PayloadTermQuery's on term `humpty` and `dumpty`. Then, finally, we override the `scorePayload` method:

```
public float scorePayload(int doc, int start, int end, BytesRef
payload) {
    float val = PayloadHelper.decodeFloat(payload.bytes);
    if (start == 0 || start == 1) {
        return val * 0.1f;
    }
    return val * 100f;
}
```

Note that in the override, we check the start position, and penalize documents where the term is in position *0* or *1* by reducing their Payload to a tenth of its value. The term in other positions is awarded with 100 times the Payload value. Here is what the final output looks like:

```
24.667135: Couldn't put Humpty together again.
0.11240285: Humpty Dumpty sat on a wall,
0.11240285: Humpty Dumpty had a great fall.
```

Note that the first and second sentences' scores are significantly less because Query terms exist in position *0* and *1*; hence, the lower score.

For the next override, we will have to change our setup a little bit to ensure the `sloppyFreq` method is being called. The change is to add quotes around the query to make it a `PhraseQuery` and call `setPhraseSlop` in QueryParser to allow for sloppy phrase match:

```
queryParser.setPhraseSlop(1);
Query query = queryParser.parse("\"humpty dumpty\"");
```

Also, here is the override:

```
public float sloppyFreq(int distance) {
    if (distance == 0) {
        return super.sloppyFreq(distance) * 100;
    }
    return super.sloppyFreq(distance);
}
```

In this example, we favor the exact match in phrase matching. The score is a boost by a factor of 100 when the distance between the terms is zero. This code will produce the following result:

```
11.43841: Humpty Dumpty sat on a wall,
10.008609: Humpty Dumpty had a great fall.
```

The last override is the `tf(float)` method. This method calculates the score based on term's frequency in a document. Here is the override:

```
public float tf(float freq) {
    if (freq > 1f) {
        return super.tf(freq) * 100;
    }
    return super.tf(freq);
}
```

This method favors term's frequency greater than *1*. In our setup, since none of the terms appear more than once in the documents, running with this override will return the same results as without it.

There's more...

Outside of the default TFIDFSimilarity scoring model, Lucene also provides other implementations out of the box. In this section, we will go over these models at high level to give you a perspective of what scoring options are available. Here is the list of the additional scoring models:

- The BM25 model
- The language model
- The divergence from randomness model
- The information-based model

The BM25 model

This model is usually referred to as **Okapi BM25** because it was first implemented in the Okapi information retrieval system. BM25 is one of the most developed models and is widely used in web search engines. It's a probabilistic model matching query terms to each matching document to calculate the document's relevance to the query. The computation is based on the frequency of query terms that appear in a document. You may be wondering if BM25 is similar to TF-IDF (implemented in Lucene's default Similarity). They are actually quite different as BM25 emphasizes comparing query terms to documents, while TF-IDF is a term-based scoring method; although in TFIDFSimilarity, document scoring is wrapped up and handled by the vector space model.

The language model

The language model takes a different approach. Instead of calculating a document's relevance to a query, it generates a probabilistic model from each document and calculates the score based on the probability of the document's model to generate the query. This is similar to the idea that when users search for specific documents, users usually try to come up with the most relevant terms contained in the documents for the query. The documents with the highest probability of generating the query terms would score higher.

The divergence from randomness model

This model is based on the hypothesis that the rarer the query term is in a document collection, the higher the probability that the term is of high relevance to the document. Say, if the query term frequency within a document is high, but the term frequency against the entire collection is low, where the two terms' frequencies diverge, the model would conclude that the term is of high relevance to the document. On the other hand, if the term also has a high-term frequency in the collection, then the term is not particularly important or relevant to the document and would have a lower score. Since term frequency in a collection depends on what goes into the model and can change overtime as the index grows, the distribution of terms is not exactly predictable, and hence is considered as a random distribution.

The information-based Model

The Information-based model shares some similarities with the language model and divergence from randomness model where both the individual document and collection are analyzed as part of the scoring components. The model is based around modeling informativeness of terms in the document and collection. The model considers that the documents with higher query term frequency get a higher score than documents with less term frequency. The incremental gain in score in high query term frequency diminishes as frequency gets higher and higher. The model also favors shorter documents compared to longer ones as longer documents dilute the term's relevancy. It also penalizes terms that appear in many documents because these terms are common and cannot be uniquely associated with a specific topic.

Implementing the BM25 model

Let's take a look at how we use the BM25 model in Lucene. Lucene implements this model as BM25Similarity. We can start using this model as simply as instantiating it with default parameters. The constructor accepts two parameters for tuning. The first parameter controls nonlinear term frequency normalization. Its default value is 1.2. The second parameter controls to what degree a document length normalizes the `tf` values.

How to do It...

Here we have our sample code to demonstrate how to use BM25Similarity;

```
StandardAnalyzer analyzer = new StandardAnalyzer();
Directory directory = new RAMDirectory();
IndexWriterConfig config =
  new IndexWriterConfig(Version.LATEST, analyzer);
BM25Similarity similarity =
  new BM25Similarity(1.2f, 0.75f);
config.setSimilarity(similarity);
IndexWriter indexWriter =
  new IndexWriter(directory, config);
Document doc = new Document();
TextField textField =
  new TextField("content", "", Field.Store.YES);
String[] contents = {"Humpty Dumpty sat on a wall,",
    "Humpty Dumpty had a great fall. " +
    "All the king's horses and all the king's men",
    "All the king's horses and all the king's men",
    "Couldn't put Humpty together again."};
for (String content : contents) {
  textField.setStringValue(content);
  doc.removeField("content");
  doc.add(textField);
  indexWriter.addDocument(doc);
}
indexWriter.commit();
IndexReader indexReader = DirectoryReader.open(directory);
IndexSearcher indexSearcher =
  new IndexSearcher(indexReader);
indexSearcher.setSimilarity(similarity);
QueryParser queryParser =
  new QueryParser("content", analyzer);
Query query = queryParser.parse("humpty");
TopDocs topDocs = indexSearcher.search(query, 100);
for (ScoreDoc scoreDoc : topDocs.scoreDocs) {
  doc = indexReader.document(scoreDoc.doc);
  System.out.println(scoreDoc.score + ": " +
    doc.getField("content").stringValue());
}
```

How it works...

Note that in this setup, we made the second sentence longer. This is so we can show how the length of a document can affect scoring. By running this code as it is, we will get this result:

```
0.42327404: Humpty Dumpty sat on a wall,
0.38780686: Couldn't put Humpty together again.
0.22321452: Humpty Dumpty had a great fall. All the king's horses and
all the king's men
```

If you change either of the parameters in BM25 Similarity's constructor to 0, you will effectively disable the algorithm. You will get matched results in the order they were added to the index and each document's score would be identical in our test scenario:

```
0.35667494: Humpty Dumpty sat on a wall,
0.35667494: Humpty Dumpty had a great fall. All the king's horses and
all the king's men
0.35667494: Couldn't put Humpty together again.
```

Now, let's try changing just the first parameter from 1.2 to 100. This should exaggerate the term frequency normalization, which in turn should exaggerate scoring. Here is the result:

```
0.4992689: Humpty Dumpty sat on a wall,
0.41751385: Couldn't put Humpty together again.
0.17104246: Humpty Dumpty had a great fall. All the king's horses and
all the king's men
```

Note that the order of the documents did not change and the first couple of results have higher scores. The last document has a lower score due to its length, which is significantly longer than other documents.

Let's revert the changes and try changing just the second parameter from 0.75 to 100 in order to control document length normalization. The change in the result is more drastic because we change the model's behavior to value longer documents more. Here is the result:

```
0.004418654: Humpty Dumpty had a great fall. All the king's horses and
all the king's men
-0.017852472: Humpty Dumpty sat on a wall,
-0.036757033: Couldn't put Humpty together again.
```

Implementing the language model

Lucene implemented two language models, LMDirichletSimilarity and LMJelinekMercerSimilarity, based on different distribution smoothing methods. Smoothing is a technique that adds a constant weight so that the zero query term frequency on partially matched documents does not result in a zero score where it's useless in ranking. We will look at these two implementations and see how their weight distributions affect scoring.

How to do it...

We will take a look at LMDirichletSimilarity first and we will reuse our test case from the previous section, but will revert the extended second sentence input:

```
StandardAnalyzer analyzer = new StandardAnalyzer();
Directory directory = new RAMDirectory();
IndexWriterConfig config = new IndexWriterConfig(Version.LATEST,
  analyzer);
LMDirichletSimilarity similarity = new
  LMDirichletSimilarity(2000);
config.setSimilarity(similarity);
IndexWriter indexWriter = new IndexWriter(directory, config);
Document doc = new Document();
TextField textField = new TextField("content", "", Field.Store.YES);
String[] contents = {"Humpty Dumpty sat on a wall,",
  "Humpty Dumpty had a great fall.",
  "All the king's horses and all the king's men",
  "Couldn't put Humpty together again."};
for (String content : contents) {
  textField.setStringValue(content);
  doc.removeField("content");
    doc.add(textField);
    indexWriter.addDocument(doc);
}
indexWriter.commit();
IndexReader indexReader = DirectoryReader.open(directory);
IndexSearcher indexSearcher = new IndexSearcher(indexReader);
indexSearcher.setSimilarity(similarity);
QueryParser queryParser = new QueryParser("content", analyzer);
Query query = queryParser.parse("humpty dumpty");
TopDocs topDocs = indexSearcher.search(query, 100);
for (ScoreDoc scoreDoc : topDocs.scoreDocs) {
  doc = indexReader.document(scoreDoc.doc);
  System.out.println(scoreDoc.score + ": " +
    doc.getField("content").stringValue());
}
```

The default value μ for LMDirichletSimilarity is *2000*. Note that the query has changed to `"humpty dumpty"`. We can pass in different values to see how the scoring differs. Let's run this code as it is; we will see the following results:

```
0.0021194727: Humpty Dumpty sat on a wall,
8.977467E-4: Humpty Dumpty had a great fall.
1.2710997E-5: Couldn't put Humpty together again.
```

Now, let's reduce the value to 200. The scoring should result as follows:

```
0.020707529: Humpty Dumpty sat on a wall,
0.0087386025: Humpty Dumpty had a great fall.
1.2429726E-4: Couldn't put Humpty together again.
```

The scoring is significantly lowered by a factor of 10 and the gaps between each rank roughly follow the same scale. The changes in scoring are somewhat linear. Staying with the default value at 2000 should suffice for most cases. Now, let's see how document length affects scoring. Let's revert μ to 2000 and add one more word to the first sentence so now it reads `"Humpty Dumpty sat on a wall, something"`. Here is the result:

```
0.0011885217: Humpty Dumpty sat on a wall, something
0.0011885217: Humpty Dumpty had a great fall.
1.3742637E-4: Couldn't put Humpty together again.
```

Note that the scoring between the first and second sentence is identical. This shows that the document length is a significant factor in this model's scoring.

In the second model, LMJelinekMercerSimilarity, it accepts a λ value as float in its constructor to tune the model. We will replace the similarity instantiation line to use LMJelinekMercerSimilarity instead. Let's try 0.01 as λ. It will produce the following result:

```
10.035212: Humpty Dumpty sat on a wall,
9.505177: Humpty Dumpty had a great fall.
4.6099925: Couldn't put Humpty together again.
```

Now, let's try changing it to 0.99. We will see the following:

```
0.03069269: Humpty Dumpty sat on a wall,
0.023542093: Humpty Dumpty had a great fall.
0.010099145: Couldn't put Humpty together again.
```

Note that the change in scoring between 0.01 and 0.99 is nonlinear. Let's examine how document length affects result. Let's change the first sentence by adding one word at the end so it becomes "`Humpty Dumpty sat on a wall, something`" and revert λ to 0.01. It will produce the following:

```
9.597424: Humpty Dumpty sat on a wall, something
9.597424: Humpty Dumpty had a great fall.
4.65606: Couldn't put Humpty together again.
```

Note that we get a similar behavior from our test in LMDirichletSimilarity where the first and second sentences now return the same score.

Having seen both the language models in action, you may be wondering how to choose the best value to tune these models. The answer is complicated because these models are based on a complex statistical theory. It's difficult to tell from the implementation point of view what tuning value is best for your scenario. The best approach would be experimentation with test data and to try different values to find something that gives you the best results.

Implementing the divergence from randomness model

In Lucene, divergence from randomness model is implemented as DFRSimilarity. It's made up of three components: **BasicModel**, **AfterEffect**, and **Normalization**. BasicModel is a model of information content, AfterEffect is the first normalization, and Normalization is second (length) normalization. Here is an excerpt from Lucene's Javadoc on DFRSimilarity's components:

1. **BasicModel**: This is a basic model of information content:

   - `BasicModelBE`: This is the limiting form of Bose-Einstein
   - `BasicModelG`: This is the geometric approximation of Bose-Einstein
   - `BasicModelP`: This is the Poisson approximation of the Binomial
   - `BasicModelD`: This is the divergence approximation of the Binomial
   - `BasicModelIn`: This is the inverse document frequency
   - `BasicModelIne`: This is the inverse expected document frequency (mixture of Poisson and IDF)
   - `BasicModelIF`: This is the inverse term frequency (approximation of I(ne))

2. **AfterEffect**: This is the first normalization of information gain:

- ❑ `AfterEffectL`: This is Laplace's law of succession
- ❑ `AfterEffectB`: This is the ratio of two Bernoulli processes
- ❑ `AfterEffect.NoAfterEffect`: This indicates that there is no first normalization

3. **Normalization**: This is the second (length) normalization:

- ❑ `NormalizationH1`: uniform distribution of term frequency
- ❑ `NormalizationH2`: Term frequency density inversely related to length
- ❑ `NormalizationH3`: Term frequency normalization provided by Dirichlet prior
- ❑ `NormalizationZ`: Term frequency normalization provided by a Zipfian relation
- ❑ `Normalization.NoNormalization`: No second normalization

How to do It...

Let's set up our test case:

```
StandardAnalyzer analyzer = new StandardAnalyzer();
Directory directory = new RAMDirectory();
IndexWriterConfig config = new IndexWriterConfig(Version.LATEST,
  analyzer);
DFRSimilarity similarity = new DFRSimilarity(
  new BasicModelIn(),
  new AfterEffectL(),
  new NormalizationH1());
config.setSimilarity(similarity);
IndexWriter indexWriter = new IndexWriter(directory, config);
Document doc = new Document();
TextField textField = new TextField("content", "",
  Field.Store.YES);

String[] contents = {"Humpty Dumpty sat on a wall,",
  "Humpty Dumpty had a great fall.",
  "All the king's horses and all the king's men",
  "Couldn't put Humpty together again."};
for (String content : contents) {
  textField.setStringValue(content);
  doc.removeField("content");
  doc.add(textField);
```

```
    indexWriter.addDocument(doc);
  }
  indexWriter.commit();

  IndexReader indexReader = DirectoryReader.open(directory);
  IndexSearcher indexSearcher = new IndexSearcher(indexReader);
  indexSearcher.setSimilarity(similarity);
  QueryParser queryParser = new QueryParser("content", analyzer);
  Query query = queryParser.parse("humpty dumpty");

  TopDocs topDocs = indexSearcher.search(query, 100);
  for (ScoreDoc scoreDoc : topDocs.scoreDocs) {
    doc = indexReader.document(scoreDoc.doc);
    System.out.println(scoreDoc.score + ": " +
      doc.getField("content").stringValue());
  }
```

In our test, we are using BasicModelIn (inverse document frequency), AfterEffectL (Laplace's law of succession), and NormalizationH1 (uniform distribution of term frequency).

How it works...

This code will produce the following result:

```
0.8414296: Humpty Dumpty sat on a wall,
0.74065953: Humpty Dumpty had a great fall.
0.25163758: Couldn't put Humpty together again.
```

The result is very much as expected where the shortest sentence (after removal of stop words) is ranked first. Let's now try disabling the second normalization (on document lengths) by providing `Normalization.NoNormalization` in the constructor instead. The results should be as follows:

```
0.75728655: Humpty Dumpty sat on a wall,
0.75728655: Humpty Dumpty had a great fall.
0.25728658: Couldn't put Humpty together again.
```

Note that the scores between the first and second sentences are now identical because length is not a factor anymore.

Let's try switching from a BasicModel to BasicModelIF (inverse term frequency) this time. We will get the following result:

```
1.5917058: Humpty Dumpty sat on a wall,
1.4010824: Humpty Dumpty had a great fall.
0.62600094: Couldn't put Humpty together again.
```

Note that the scoring distribution is drastically different from BasicModelIn where the gap between the second and third documents is a lot bigger.

So, the question arises again on what model to use and how to tune this similarity to suit your needs. The answer again is experimentation. You may want to try different combinations to find one that works best for your dataset.

Implementing the information-based model

The information-based model in Lucene consists of three components: **Distribution**, **Lambda**, and **Normalization**. The setup is somewhat similar to DFRSimilarity where you need to instantiate these components in its constructor. The name of the Similarity class for this model is called IBSimilarity. Here is an excerpt from Lucene's Javadoc on the components:

1. **Distribution**: This is probabilistic distribution used to model term occurrence:
   - ❑ DistributionLL: This is the Log-logistic distribution
   - ❑ DistributionSPL: This is the Smoothed power-law distribution

2. **Lambda**: This is the λw parameter of the probability distribution:
   - ❑ LambdaDF: This is the now/nor average number of documents where *w* occurs
   - ❑ LambdaTTF: This is the Fw/Nor average number of occurrences of *w* in the collection

3. **Normalization**: This is term frequency normalization:
   - ❑ NormalizationH1: In this, there is a uniform distribution of term frequency
   - ❑ NormalizationH2: In this, term frequency density is inversely related to length
   - ❑ NormalizationH3: In this, term frequency normalization is provided by Dirichlet prior
   - ❑ NormalizationZ: In this, term frequency normalization is provided by a Zipfian relation
   - ❑ Normalization.NoNormalization: In this, there is no second normalization

How to do It...

We are going to set up our test case to use DistributionSPL, LambdaDF, and NormalizationH1:

```
StandardAnalyzer analyzer = new StandardAnalyzer();
Directory directory = new RAMDirectory();
IndexWriterConfig config = new IndexWriterConfig(Version.LATEST,
analyzer);
IBSimilarity similarity = new IBSimilarity(
  new DistributionSPL(),
  new LambdaDF(),
  new NormalizationH1());
  config.setSimilarity(similarity);
  IndexWriter indexWriter = new IndexWriter(directory, config);
Document doc = new Document();
TextField textField = new TextField("content", "",
  Field.Store.YES);
String[] contents = {"Humpty Dumpty sat on a wall,",
  "Humpty Dumpty had a great fall.",
  "All the king's horses and all the king's men",
  "Couldn't put Humpty together again."};
for (String content : contents) {
    textField.setStringValue(content);
    doc.removeField("content");
    doc.add(textField);
    indexWriter.addDocument(doc);
}
indexWriter.commit();
IndexReader indexReader = DirectoryReader.open(directory);
IndexSearcher indexSearcher = new IndexSearcher(indexReader);
indexSearcher.setSimilarity(similarity);
QueryParser queryParser = new QueryParser("content", analyzer);
Query query = queryParser.parse("humpty dumpty");
TopDocs topDocs = indexSearcher.search(query, 100);
for (ScoreDoc scoreDoc : topDocs.scoreDocs) {
    doc = indexReader.document(scoreDoc.doc);
    System.out.println(scoreDoc.score + ": " +
doc.getField("content").stringValue());
}
```

How it works...

The code will produce the following result:

```
1.8361073: Humpty Dumpty sat on a wall,
1.5318649: Humpty Dumpty had a great fall.
0.7275219: Couldn't put Humpty together again.
```

Now, let's try to skip normalization by instantiating `Normalization.NoNormalization` instead. The result is as follows:

```
1.5794742: Humpty Dumpty sat on a wall,
1.5794742: Humpty Dumpty had a great fall.
0.7504883: Couldn't put Humpty together again.
```

This behaves as expected where document lengths are not considered.

Let's try a different distribution this time: DistributionLL. The result is as follows:

```
2.0669947: Humpty Dumpty sat on a wall,
1.7403756: Humpty Dumpty had a great fall.
0.7867691: Couldn't put Humpty together again.
```

Note that the scoring gaps between documents are wider now.

Experimentation is the key when choosing the right model and configuration for your dataset. Many of these models are built based on the same principle returning the most relevant documents for a given query. There are subtle differences between each approach and there are pros and cons depending on the type of data you are dealing with. However, for the most part, DefaultSimilarity should be sufficient for the majority of the implementation.

8
Introducing Elasticsearch

We have seen how Lucene can be incorporated to build a high performance search application. We have also learned that Lucene by itself is a library, as it is not intended to run as a stand-alone service. Because Lucene does not come with any user interfaces, in order to use it, we need to write some codes around the library to provide our own interfaces. The road to adapt to Lucene may not be as straightforward as using a stand-alone service, but the many customizable options Lucene provides out of the box should outweigh the burden of the initial setup. To make setup simpler and allow the user to deploy Lucene quickly, we can leverage an open source product called Elasticsearch. This provides a user interface that wraps around Lucene. It is a stand-alone server with its own facilities to manage data injection operations and searches. It also comes with all sorts of tools to manage all aspects of indexing and searching processes. We are going to cover the basic operations of Elasticsearch in this chapter and we will include the following recipes to get you started:

- ► Getting Elasticsearch
- ► Creating a new index
- ► Predefine field mappings
- ► Adding a document
- ► Deleting a document
- ► Updating a document
- ► Performing bulk indexing
- ► Searching the index
- ► Scaling Elasticsearch

Introduction

There are currently two major open source search engine projects that are based on Lucene. They are Solr and Elasticsearch; both are very capable search engines and their search/indexing performance and features are comparable. Solr has a nicer admin user interface, while Elasticsearch provides a simpler RESTful interface for its entire API. Elasticsearch has more emphasis on sharding for distributed architecture, although Solr also provides SolrCloud, which is Solr's answer to the distributed architecture. At the time of writing, the latest Elasticsearch release is a stack of **Elasticsearch**, **Logstash**, and **Kibana**. Elasticsearch is becoming a big player in data analytics, providing capability to slice and dice time-series data (for example, logs analysis by Logstash) and visualization with Kibana.

Elasticsearch accepts data in JSON format. JSON is a widely accepted data format, you can read more about it here: `http://www.json.org/`. It also has the ability to be schema-less when ingesting data. You can pass any JSON documents to Elasticsearch, and it will automatically define the appropriate schema to store the documents. This means that you do not need to define fields in advance.

Elasticsearch exposes a RESTful interface, so you can communicate with it via HTTP protocol. You can use any HTTP clients. In this chapter, we will be using CURL, a command line tool, to demonstrate interfacing with Elasticsearch. You can read more about CURL here: `http://curl.haxx.se/`.

Elasticsearch leverages HTTP methods such as PUT, GET, DELETE, and POST to organize its RESTful interface. As the names suggests, PUT is for inputting configuration and settings, GET is for retrieval, DELETE is for data removal, and POST is for data ingestion.

Getting Elasticsearch

In this section, we will look into getting and setting up Elasticsearch. The installation process is straightforward as all you need to do is extract the downloaded file into your desired location. Then, you can run it as it is with default settings to begin using the search engine. We will also install a web front plugin called Elasticsearch-head to provide a user interface to browse and interact with Elasticsearch.

Getting ready

The prerequisite to install Elasticsearch is Java 7; only Oracle's Java and OpenJDK are supported. The installation package of Elasticsearch can be found on their official site: `https://www.elastic.co/downloads`. After you have downloaded the installation package, you can extract the package into an installation location.

How to do it...

You are now actually ready to run Elasticsearch, but before we start the search engine, let's install the Elasticsearch-head plugin. You can run the following commands in command line to perform the installation in the Elasticsearch directory:

```
bin/plugin -install mobz/elasticsearch-head
```

After you run the command, you will see the following output:

```
-> Installing mobz/elasticsearch-head...
Trying https://github.com/mobz/elasticsearch-head/archive/master.zip...
Downloading ......................................................................
.................................................................................
.................................................................................
.................................................................................
.................................................................................
..................................DONE
Installed mobz/elasticsearch-head into /Users/ed/projects/
elasticsearch-1.4.4/plugins/head
Identified as a _site plugin, moving to _site structure ...
```

A new directory `plugin` should be created. If the new directory does not exist, review the installation steps and Elasticsearch's latest documentation.

To start Elasticsearch, run the following command:

```
bin/elasticsearch
```

If you are on a Linux environment, you can start Elasticsearch in the background with the `-d` switch:

```
bin/elasticsearch -d
```

After Elasticsearch is started, confirm it's running by going to the `9200` port (default port):

```
curl http://localhost:9200
```

It should return with something like the following:

```
{
  status: 200,
  name: "Analyzer",
  cluster_name: "elasticsearch",
  version: {
    number: "1.4.4",
```

```
      build_hash: "c88f77ffc81301dfa9dfd81ca2232f09588bd512",
      build_timestamp: "2015-03-01T00:00:00Z",
      build_snapshot: false,
      lucene_version: "4.10.3"
    },
    tagline: "You Know, for Search"
  }
```

This confirms that Elasticsearch is, in fact, running. Now, we will confirm if the Elastichsearch-head plugin is running properly. Open a browser and enter the following URL on the browser:

```
http://localhost:9200/_plugin/head/
```

The browser should display the following:

This shows that Elasticsearch-head is responding and can be used to interface with the Elasticsearch engine. Its functionalities should be self-explanatory. You can review the cluster, see the fields in the index, perform a search, and perform maintenance tasks using this web interface.

How it works...

The Elasticsearch team strives for simplicity when it comes down to interfacing with the engine. As you saw already, the installation and start-up of Elasticsearch couldn't be simpler. Elasticsearch is built with a pluggable architecture, so adding enhancement features can be done easily by installing plugins. The installation of Elasticsearch-head is a demonstration of how easy it is to install a plugin.

There's more...

The Elasticsearch-head plugin we just installed provides the facilities to interface with Elasticsearch on a web browser. You can read more about it here: `http://mobz.github.io/elasticsearch-head/`.

Moreover, the Elasticsearch community has built numerous plugins to extend Elasticsearch's functionalities. More plugins can be found in the following link:

```
http://www.elasticsearch.org/guide/en/elasticsearch/reference/
current/modules-plugins.html
```

Creating a new index

Before we start adding any documents to Elasticsearch, we need to create an index first. An index in Elasticsearch is basically a named space where you can ingest data. Elasticsearch supports multiple indexes, handling right out of the box. We will take advantage of it by creating our own index for our exercise.

How to do it...

Run the following command to start a new index by using the HTTP PUT method:

```
curl -XPUT 'http://localhost:9200/news/'
```

This command should return the following:

```
{"acknowledged":true}
```

If the index already exists (for example, run the above command twice), you will see the following error message:

```
{"error":"IndexAlreadyExistsException[[news] already
exists]","status":400}
```

To confirm the index is created, we can use the GET method:

```
curl -XGET 'http://localhost:9200/news/'
```

This should return the following:

```
{
  news: {
    aliases: { },
    mappings: { },
    settings: {
      index: {
        creation_date: "1425700268502",
        number_of_shards: "5",
        number_of_replicas: "1",
```

```
        version: {
            created: "1040499"
        },
        uuid: "JB2xmLhaSJO4AUnJvY_bfw"
      }
    },
    warmers: { }
  }
}
```

Now, if we go back to Elasticsearch-head (`http://localhost:9200/_plugin/head/`) on a browser, we will be able to find the new index **news** that we have just added:

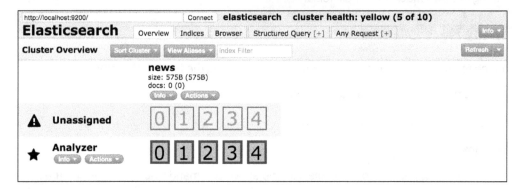

How it works...

Elasticsearch's interface is primarily HTTP-based. In this exercise, we used the HTTP PUT method to tell Elasticsearch that we are adding something to the index. The `/news/` path indicates the name of the index to be added. Note that PUT is mainly used for configuration updates.

In the second statement, we used the `GET` method to ask Elasticsearch to return the information about the index. Note that the default number of shards is 5 and default number of replicas is 1.

In the last screenshot of Elasticsearch-head, note that under the `news` index, there are two rows of numbers 0 to 4. These numbers represent shards. We specified 5 shards and 1 replica in our exercise, and we can clearly see the configuration on the screen. The green numbers represent the 5 active shards in the index. The 5 gray numbers represent the 1 replica. The replica's shards are grayed out because they are unassigned and are not active at the moment.

Predefine field mappings

A mapping is analogous to the table in a database; it contains fields that are equivalent to the columns in a table. However, a mapping is only a logical separation; it does not physically separate the data between mappings as tables do in a database. When data gets added to an index, they are all stored as documents in Lucene. Although Elasticsearch supports schema-less data ingestion, we should always predefine fields so that we know exactly what data types are mapped instead of relying on Elasticsearch to detect data types, which sometimes may produce undesired results. In this section, we will demonstrate field mappings for a news article's index.

How to do it...

We will be using the `put mapping` API to predefine fields. Here is an example:

```
curl -XPUT "localhost:9200/news/_mapping/article" -d '
{
  "article" : {
    "properties" : {
      "title" : {"type" : "string", "store" : true, "index" :
"analyzed" },
      "content": {"type" : "string", "store" : true, "index" :
"analyzed" },
      "publication_date": {"type" : "date", "store" : true, "index" :
"not_analyzed" }
    }
  }
}'
```

This should return the following output:

```
{"acknowledged":true}
```

To confirm mapping is, in fact, stored, run the following command:

```
curl -XGET "localhost:9200/news/_mapping/article"
```

This should return this JSON:

```
{
  "news" : {
    "mappings" : {
      "article" : {
```

```
        "properties" : {
          "content" : {"type":"string","store":true},
          "publication_date":{ "type":"date","store":true,
  "format":"dateOptionalTime"},
          "title":{"type":"string","store":true}
        }
      }
    }
  }
}
```

In Elasticsearch-head, under **Browser** tab, we should be able to find the three fields that we just added:

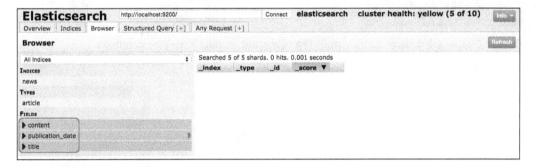

How it works....

In the first command, we used the HTTP PUT method to add a new mapping called article to the news index with three fields: title, content, and publication date. In each field, we specified the data type, whether to store the data into document, and whether to analyze field by an analyzer.

In the second command, we used HTTP GET to return the mapping definition. We can also review equivalent information in Elasticsearch-head, as shown in the preceding screenshot.

Adding a document

After index and mapping are created, we can begin sending data to Elasticsearch for indexing. We can use either HTTP PUT or POST to submit data. The difference between these two methods is that with PUT, we need to specify a unique ID, whereas with POST, Elasticsearch will automatically generate an ID for us. Here is the general URL format to submit a document:

```
http://<host>:<port>/<index>/<mapping>
```

Both methods accept data in JSON format. In our scenario, the JSON format should be in a flat key value pair structure.

How to do it...

Let's look at an example. We will use both HTTP methods to submit news articles to our index.

Using HTTP PUT:

```
curl -XPUT 'http://localhost:9200/news/article/1' -d '
{
    "title" : "Europe stocks tumble on political fears , PMI data" ,
    "publication_date" : "2012-03-30",
    "content" : "LONDON (MarketWatch)-European stock markets tumbled
to a three-month low on Monday, driven by steep losses for banks and
resource firms after weak purchasing-managers index readings from
China and Europe. At the same time, political tensions in France and
the Netherlands fuelled fears of further euro-zone turmoil"
}'
```

This should return the following:

```
{"_index":"news","_type":"article","_id":"1","_
version":1,"created":true}
```

Using HTTP POST:

```
curl -XPOST 'http://localhost:9200/news/article/' -d '
{
    "title" : "Dow Rises, Gains 1.5% on Week" ,
    "publication_date" : "2012-03-03",
    "content" : "Solid quarterly results from consumer-oriented
stocks including Amazon.com AMZN +15.75% overshadowed data on slowing
economic growth, pushing benchmarks to their biggest weekly advance
since mid-March."
}'
```

This should return the following:

```
{"_index":"news","_type":"article","_id":"AUv7IqVcy3AfbdbmyrgB","_
version":1,"created":true}
```

Now, let's take a look at Elasticsearch-head:

How it works...

In the PUT method, we added `/1` at the end of the URL to specify our own unique id. After the document is accepted, it returns a created confirmation where `_id` is 1. In the POST method, note that we submitted an article without any id. The created confirmation now returns a new auto generated id `AUv7IqVcy3AfbdbmyrgB`. As expected, the articles are added as documents in Lucene. We can confirm the two documents that exist by using Elasticsearch-head, as shown in the preceding screenshot.

Deleting a document

The `delete` API allows you to delete a document by id. When documents are added to the index, an id (`_id field`) that is either supplied by source data or automatically generated, is always assigned. Every document in the index has to have an `_id` value as it's used to uniquely identify a document within an index and type. The delete API can be triggered by the HTTP DELETE method.

How to do it...

Here is a command to delete a document where the id is 1 in the news index, under type to article:

```
curl -XDELETE 'http://localhost:9200/news/article/1'
```

If the document exists, it should return a message like the following:

```
{"found":true,"_index":"news","_type":"article","_id":"1","_version":2}
```

Otherwise, it would say `not found`:

```
{"found":false,"_index":"news","_type":"article","_id":"1","_version":1}
```

How it works...

The DELETE HTTP method triggers the delete API. In our example, we specified the index as news and type as article in the URL and document id (_id field) as 1. We can verify the document has been deleted by going into Elasticsearch-head.

 Note that **_id** is only unique within an index and type. The same **_id** can be assigned to multiple documents of different types. This field is different from DocId.

Updating a document

The updated API allows you to add/update fields in a document. The action can be triggered by using the HTTP PUT or POST method. A document can be specified by their ids (_id field).

How to do it...

Let's assume that we have an existing document in our news article index, in which id is 1 and title is "Europe stocks tumble on political fears, PMI data". We will submit an update action to update title to "Europe stocks tumble on political fears, PMI data | STOCK NEWS".

Here is a PUT method example:

```
curl -XPUT 'http://localhost:9200/news/article/1' -d '
{
    "title" : "Europe stocks tumble on political fears, PMI data |
STOCK NEWS"
}'
```

If successful, it should return the following:

```
{"_index":"news","_type":"article","_id":"1","_
version":2,"created":false}
```

Here is a POST method example:

```
curl -XPOST 'http://localhost:9200/news/article/1/_update' -d '
{ "doc" : {
    "title" : "Europe stocks tumble on political fears, PMI data |
STOCK NEWS"
  }
}'
```

If successful, it should return the following:

```
{"_index":"news","_type":"article","_id":"1","_version":7}
```

How it works...

Note that we used HTTP PUT to trigger an update, and we specified the document by `/news/article/1`. The updated field is specified in JSON. Note that this is a similar action as adding a document to an index. If id does not exist, this command will create a new document with that id. Because this is similar to adding a new document to the index, this command basically tells the engine to add/replace the document with what's provided in JSON. In this scenario, the title is renamed, but the `publication_date` and content fields are wiped because we did not specify values for these two fields.

The second example with the POST method allows for a partial document update. We specified a value for **title** only, and this will be the only field in the document that gets updated.

Performing bulk indexing

Elasticsearch supports bulk operation to load/update data to the index. The advantage of bulk update is that it reduces the number of HTTP calls, which will in turn increase throughput by the reduction of turnarounds between calls. When using the bulk API, we should use a file to store bulk data to prepare for an upload. In CURL, we can use the `--data-binary` flag to upload a file, instead of the `-d` plain. This is because in bulk mode, a newline character is treated as a record delimiter, which means no pretty print JSON.

Bulk API supports most update operations and can be broken down into four types of actions: index, create, delete, and update. Index and create serve a similar purpose; you can use either one to insert a document. The action composed of two rows: a row for action and metadata, and a row for source (for example, a document we want to insert). Delete has the same semantics as delete API and it does not require a source. Update's syntax is similar to index/create and it can be used to update an existing document.

From Elasticsearch's documentation, they specified bulk data format, as follows:

```
action_and_meta_data\n
optional_source\n
action_and_meta_data\n
optional_source\n
action_and_meta_data\n
optional_source\n
```

The bulk API can be triggered by using the `/_bulk` endpoint in the URL. There are three ways to initiate bulk operations: `/_bulk`, `/{index}/_bulk` or `/{index}/{type}/_bulk`. If you don't specify an index and type, you will have to specify it in the bulk action. We will show you what the actions look like.

How to do it...

We will demonstrate bulk data load actions with the following:

```
{ index: { "_index" : "news", "_type" : "article", "_id" : "2" } }
{ "title" : "Debt crisis: as it happened, April 25, 2012" ,
"publication_date" : "2012-03-23", "content" : "US Federal Reserve
raises growth forecasts and says will keep interest rates low until
2014, as chairman Ben Bernanke says the bank remains prepared to do
more to help economy" }
{ index: { "_index" : "news", "_type" : "article" } }
{ "title" : "Stocks: 2013 is one for the record books." ,
"publication_date" : "2013-12-31", "content" : "The Dow Jones
industrial average (INDU) had its best year since 1998. The blue chip
index gained 26.5% this year, hitting 52 all-time highs along the way.
And the Nasdaq (COMP) surged 38%, marking its best year since 2009." }
```

The above should be saved to a file so that it can be referenced in the CURL.

Here is the CURL command:

```
curl -XPOST 'http://localhost:9200/news/article/_bulk' --data-binary @
file.txt
```

This is assuming the above actions are saved into a file called `file.txt`. If the command runs successfully, it should return the following:

```
{"took":9,"errors":false,"items":[{"index":{"_index":"news","_type
":"article","_id":"2","_version":1,"status":201}},{"create":{"_ind
ex":"news","_type":"article","_id":"AUwGYt61qOavQVqFNDEW","_versio
n":1,"status":201}}]}
```

Here is another bulk example to update a document, changing *Document 2's* title to *NO TITLE*:

```
{ update: { "_index" : "news", "_type" : "article", "_id" : "2" } }
{ "doc" : { "title" : "NO TITLE" } }
```

This should return the following:

```
{"took":12,"errors":false,"items":[{"update":{"_index":"news","_ty
pe":"article","_id":"2","_version":2,"status":200}}]}
```

Here is another example to delete a document; this time, we are deleting `Document 2`:

```
{ delete: { "_index" : "news", "_type" : "article", "_id" : "2" } }
```

The response value should be as follows:

```
{"took":1,"errors":false,"items":[{"delete":{"_index":"news","_typ
e":"article","_id":"2","_version":3,"status":200,"found":true}}]}
```

How it works...

In the first example, we had two index actions to create two documents. Note that each action comprises of two rows. The first row is for action and metadata, and the second row is for the document. There is also a slight difference between these two index actions. The first one has a specified _id, while the second one doesn't have one. You can see it in the result with two responses. The first result confirmed a document with id 2 that is added, and the second result confirmed the addition of a document with an autogenerated id AUwGYt61qOavQVqFNDEW.

In the second example, we submitted an update action to change the article id 2's title field to "NO TITLE". Note that JSON is similar to what you would submit to the delete API.

In the third example, we submitted a delete action to remove the article id 2 from the index. Note that the found attribute is in the result. This tells you whether the record was found.

Searching the index

Elasticsearch has a flexible search interface; it allows you to search across multiple indexes and types, or limited to a specific index and/or type. The search interface supports the URL search with a query string as a parameter, or using a request body in a JSON format, in which you can use Elasticsearch's Query **DSL** (**domain-specific language**) to specify search components. We will go over both these approaches in this section.

How to do it...

Let's look at the following examples:

```
curl -XGET 'http://localhost:9200/news/article/_search?q=monday'

curl -XGET 'http://localhost:9200/news,news2/article/_search?q=monday'

curl -XGET 'http://localhost:9200/news/article,article2/_search?q=monday'

curl -XGET 'http://localhost:9200/news/_search?q=monday'

curl -XGET 'http://localhost:9200/_search?q=monday'
```

Each command represents different demonstrations of URI-based searches. We can in any combination of indexes and types. Assuming that we do have an existing document in the index with the term `monday`, we can expect to see a result that is similar to the following:

```
{"took":37,"timed_out":false,"_shards":{"total":5,"successful":5,
"failed":0},"hits":{"total":1,"max_score":0.038356602,"hits":[{"_
index":"news","_type":"article","_id":"1","_score":0.038356602,"_
source":{"title":"Europe stocks tumble on political fears, PMI data
| STOCK NEWS","publication_date":"2012-03-30","content":"LONDON
(MarketWatch)-European stock markets tumbled to a three-month low on
Monday, driven by steep losses for banks and resource firms after weak
purchasing-managers index readings from China and Europe. At the same
time, political tensions in France and the Netherlands fuelled fears
of further euro-zone turmoil"}}]}}
```

Here is an example of searching by a request body:

```
curl -XGET 'http://localhost:9200/news/article/_search' -d '{
  "query" : {
    "term" : { "content" : "monday" }
  }
}'
```

Under the same perquisites, this query should return something similar to the results from the last test.

How it works...

The search API follows the same semantics as other APIs for which you can specify one or more indexes and types. As shown in the example, the endpoint for search is `/_search`.

In the first example, in which we demonstrated the URI-based searches, we can see an index and type can be specified in one or many forms. The `q` parameter is to specify a query string. The search result also shows the total matching documents; see the `total` attribute.

In the second example, in which we used a request body to submit a search query, we specified a term query to match `monday` on the content field.

There's more...

The request body based search only demonstrated a term query. Elasticsearch can support many different query types such as Boolean Query and DisMax Query. They all can be found in Elasticsearch's Query DSL page:

```
http://www.elastic.co/guide/en/elasticsearch/reference/current/query-
dsl-queries.html
```

Scaling Elasticsearch

The main selling point of Elasticsearch is its simplicity to scale. Even by running it in a default setting, it immediately begins to showcase its scalability ability with an index of 5 shards and 1 replica (default index settings). The name Elastic in Elasticsearch refers to its clustering flexibility. You can easily scale up Elasticsearch by adding more machines into the mix in order to instantly increase capacity. It also includes the facility to handle automatic failover, so that planning for scalable and high availability architecture is greatly simplified.

To better comprehend Elasticsearch's scaling strategy, you will need to understand three main concepts: **sharding**, **replica**, and **clustering**. These are the core concepts that help drive elasticity in Elasticsearch.

A shard is a single Lucene index instance; it represents a slice of a bigger dataset. Sharding is a data partitioning strategy to make a large dataset more manageable. When dealing with an ever-growing dataset, at some point, single instance hardware will eventually become inadequate to handle the data volume. Obviously, hardware can be upgraded in order to improve performance. This is called vertical scaling and is usually one of the first things that comes to mind when dealing with the performance issue. However, there is an upper limit on what you can upgrade on a single machine. Generally, scaling vertically and upgrading hardware is simpler than scaling horizontally, data partitioning, and adding more machines. This is because partitioning data on a system that has not been provisioned to do so will require a
lot of architectural planning and consideration. It's a complex issue.

Elasticsearch's sharding capability is an elegant solution to solve the horizontal scaling challenge. Elasticsearch can be configured easily to index on any number of shards. The default sharding strategy is based on the **_id** field. It's almost always advisable to think of your own sharding strategy to bring out the most optimal performance. For example, if your application is reporting systems in which a user can only see his/her own data, sharding by user id will be ideal. This is because a user's actions will only need access to one shard, instead of accessing all shards all the time.

A replica is a copy of an index. A replication scheme is used to maintain data integrity between a live index and replica. In Elasticsearch, replica can be used to serve read requests, help to increase throughput, and allow for failover when one of the machines fails in a cluster. It's highly recommended to always maintain one or more replicas in order to ensure data safety and maintain uptime for your application.

An Elasticsearch cluster consists of a number of nodes. A node is a single Elasticsearch instance and it contains one or more shards/replicas. Elasticsearch is a peer-to-peer based system in which the cluster as a whole is self-aware. When a node enters into a cluster, the cluster can begin to leverage the new node to store shards/replicas. With replicas, a node may fail at any point, and the cluster will reroute traffics to avoid the affected nodes. The number of node failures a cluster can sustain will depend on the replica configuration. There is also a master node that oversees and manages operations. Had it failed, that master node can also be reelected from the remaining nodes. After all, Elasticsearch's appeal is its clustering capability and easiness to manage load balancing and fault tolerance. With all that said, Elasticsearch can maintain a cluster, handling failover automatically without any user intervention.

How to do it...

Setting up a cluster is easy. For simplicity's sake, we will start a cluster under the same install directory. All you have to do is start Elasticsearch twice. The second instance will automatically move the port number up by 1 from 9200 to 9201. Elasticsearch uses multicast to detect node; if you are on a company network in which multicast may be disabled, you may need to unplug from your network to do this test.

Here is what you will see on the first instance startup:

```
version[1.4.4], pid[1490], build[c88f77f/2015-02-19T13:05:36Z]
initializing ...
loaded [], sites [head]
initialized
starting ...
bound_address {inet[/0:0:0:0:0:0:0:0:9300]}, publish_address
{inet[local/127.0.0.1:9300]}
elasticsearch/Y7usoZ3rSGOljrW7C-Si7Q
Infamnia] new_master [Infamnia][Y7usoZ3rSGOljrW7C-Si7Q][local]
[inet[local/127.0.0.1:9300]], reason: zen-disco-join (elected_as_
master)
bound_address {inet[/0:0:0:0:0:0:0:0:9200]}, publish_address
{inet[local/127.0.0.1:9200]}
started
recovered [1] indices into cluster_state
added {[Diamondhead][cHPVt8TpSaybb_0EoD01bA][local]
[inet[/127.0.0.1:9301]],}, reason: zen-disco-receive(join
from node[[Diamondhead][cHPVt8TpSaybb_0EoD01bA][local]
[inet[/127.0.0.1:9301]]])
```

Here is the second instance logs:

```
version[1.4.4], pid[1500], build[c88f77f/2015-02-19T13:05:36Z]
initializing ...
loaded [], sites [head]
initialized
starting ...
bound_address {inet[/0:0:0:0:0:0:0:9301]}, publish_address
{inet[local/127.0.0.1:9301]}
elasticsearch/cHPVt8TpSaybb_0EoD01bA
detected_master [Infamnia][Y7usoZ3rSGOljrW7C-Si7Q][local]
[inet[/127.0.0.1:9300]], added {[Infamnia][Y7usoZ3rSGOljrW7C-
Si7Q][local][inet[/127.0.0.1:9300]],}, reason: zen-disco-
receive(from master [[Infamnia][Y7usoZ3rSGOljrW7C-Si7Q][local]
[inet[/127.0.0.1:9300]]])
bound_address {inet[/0:0:0:0:0:0:0:9201]}, publish_address
{inet[local/127.0.0.1:9201]}
started
```

Note that the second instance detected the master node and joined the cluster. You can also find a secondary node that entered the cluster from the first instance's logs.

This is what the cluster looks like in Elasticsearch-head:

How it works...

As mentioned earlier, Elasticsearch is very capable in balancing nodes all on its own, without user intervention. A master node oversees all the nodes in a cluster and when a node fails, the master node will be able to promote a replica shard into an active index for writes. Once a replacement node enters into the cluster, the master node will begin to restore balance by placing replica and primary shard back into the node. Again, this is all done without having anyone to trigger the process.

In our scenario, we used the default settings of 5 shards and 1 replica for our node. We left the default name for the cluster as `elasticsearch`. When the first instance started, it sets up the shards, but with no replica. When the second instance started, it discovered the master node in the `elasticsearch` cluster and joined the cluster. The first instance detected a new node and began assigning replica shards into the second instance.

You may notice that there are some interesting names for nodes. The names are picked by Elasticsearch if you don't specify a node name in the configuration.

There's more...

We only had a glimpse at Elasticsearch's clustering capability. There are a lot of options to customize a cluster to suit any needs. You can find more information about Elasticsearch's sharding/clustering capability here:

```
http://www.elastic.co/guide/en/elasticsearch/reference/current/index.
html
```

9
Extending Lucene with Modules

In this chapter, we will cover the following recipes:

- ▶ Exploring spatial search
- ▶ Implementing joins
- ▶ Performing faceting
- ▶ Implementing grouping
- ▶ Employing autosuggest
- ▶ Implementing highlighting

Introduction

So far, we have explored Lucene's core functionalities and learned how to customize Lucene's core components. However, we haven't yet learnt any extension libraries that expand beyond the core features. In this chapter, we will discover the add-on features in Lucene and demonstrate how these features work and how to leverage these new functionalities effectively. We will cover the following features: spatial search, joins, faceting, grouping, autosuggest, and highlighting.

Exploring spatial search

Spatial search provides the ability to search by location data. This is also called geo-spatial search. We usually leverage this type of search to look for things within a certain location proximity. It's very useful in map applications where most of the searches are about searching nearby places. Lucene provides this feature by incorporating another open source project called Spatial4j. This offers utilities for shape and distance calculation. Lucene uses these utilities to generate indexable fields to perform query calculations.

When dealing with spatial search, there are several considerations. Are we indexing points or shapes? What kind of shapes are we indexing? Can a document contain more than one point/shape? What kind of query is supported? There is no one solution that fits all in spatial search.

Lucene provides four built-in spatial strategies to help handle various types of spatial search requirements:

▶ **BBoxStrategy**: This strategy permits indexing and searching by shapes (rectangles in particular) by storing coordinates as numeric fields. Basically, a match is when the search rectangle intersects with any rectangles in the index. This can be useful on basic area search where you want to find all the matching locations within a specified rectangle boundary.

Here is a diagram that depicts what matches look like:

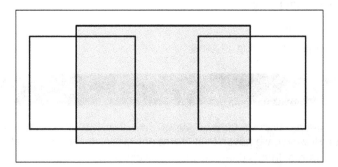

In this case, the shaded rectangle is our search query and the two intersecting rectangles are matches.

▶ **PointVectorStrategy**: As the name suggests, this strategy indexes points in *x* and *y* coordinates. Unlike BBoxStrategy, this strategy only indexes points rather than shapes. However, index can be queried by rectangle or circle shapes. A match is when a point is found within a rectangle or circle.

Here is a diagram of this strategy:

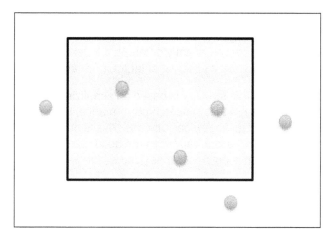

In this scenario, the points within the rectangles are matches.

- ▶ **PrefixTreeStrategy**: This is an abstract class to perform fast approximate spatial search. It only supports shape intersection searches. The two subclasses are:
  - ❑ **RecursivePrefixTreeStrategy**: This strategy is based on PrefixTreeStrategy with the support for handling nonpoint shapes.
  - ❑ **TermQueryPrefixTreeStrategy**: This strategy leverages TermFilter for filtering indexed point shapes only.

Here is a diagram that shows what PrefixTreeStrategy does:

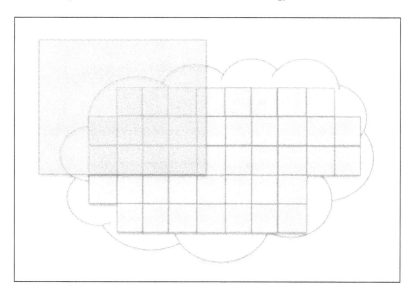

Note that this strategy approximates arbitrary shapes by using a grid of smaller shapes at an index time. This method basically allows the strategy to support any shapes. A match is when a searching query shape intersects with any shapes in the index. The preceding diagram is reflective of RecursivePrefixTreeStrategy. TermQueryPrefixTreeStrategy is slightly different; it indexes points instead of shapes for closer approximation at the expense of larger index and slower query.

▶ **SerializedDVStrategy**: This strategy is based on serializing the shape stored in BinaryDocValues so it's not fast in search performance, but would be useful in high precision per-document geometry calculations. This is not exactly a spatial index, as a search in this strategy will essentially scan the documents and calculate intersections per document. Precision is high as it is as good as the geometry that's stored in BinaryDocValues.

Getting ready...

First, we need to acquire the spatial search library. We will need the following dependency in Maven:

```
<dependency>
    <groupId>org.apache.lucene</groupId>
    <artifactId>lucene-spatial</artifactId>
    <version>VERSION</version>
</dependency>
```

How to do it...

Here is a sample implementation for performing both indexing and searching with spatial search using BBoxStrategy:

```
StandardAnalyzer analyzer = new StandardAnalyzer();
Directory directory = new RAMDirectory();
IndexWriterConfig config = new
  IndexWriterConfig(Version.LATEST, analyzer);
IndexWriter indexWriter = new IndexWriter(directory, config);
Document doc = new Document();
SpatialContext spatialContext = SpatialContext.GEO;
BBoxStrategy bBoxStrategy = new BBoxStrategy(spatialContext,
  "rectangle");
```

```
Rectangle rectangle = spatialContext.makeRectangle(1.0d,
  5.0d, 1.0d, 5.0d);
Field[] fields =
  bBoxStrategy.createIndexableFields(rectangle);
for (Field field : fields) {
  doc.add(field);
}
doc.add(new StringField("name", "Rectangle 1",
  Field.Store.YES));
indexWriter.addDocument(doc);
indexWriter.commit();
IndexReader indexReader = DirectoryReader.open(directory);
IndexSearcher indexSearcher = new IndexSearcher(indexReader);
Rectangle rectangle2 = spatialContext.makeRectangle(2.0d,
  4.0d, 0.0d, 4.0d);
SpatialArgs spatialArgs = new
  SpatialArgs(SpatialOperation.Intersects, rectangle2);
Query query = bBoxStrategy.makeQuery(spatialArgs);
TopDocs topDocs = indexSearcher.search(query, 10);
System.out.println("Total hits: " + topDocs.totalHits);
for (ScoreDoc scoreDoc : topDocs.scoreDocs) {
    doc = indexReader.document(scoreDoc.doc);
    System.out.println(scoreDoc.score + ": " +
  doc.getField("name").stringValue());
}
```

How it works...

In this test code, we set up Lucene as usual with a StandardAnalyzer, RAMDirectory, and IndexWriter. Then, we set up a SpatialContext to be used in SpatialStrategy. We used the general GEO context in `SpatialContext` as this context is suitable for all the implemented SpatialStrategy classes. We picked BBoxStrategy to search by rectangle.

We added one document into the index for indexing and search by another rectangle. To make the rectangle indexable, we called `createIndexableFields` in BBoxStrategy to generate a list of fields to be added to a Lucene document. If you step through this code and examine the fields, you will find that four fields are generated for the coordinates that are used to create the rectangle. The spatial operation for comparison is intersects. Note that we specified spatial operation as part of SpatialArgs, which is to be passed on to BBoxStrategy to generate a proper query object. The `makeQuery` method will create the right kind of query for spatial search.

Here is a diagram of what the shapes look like:

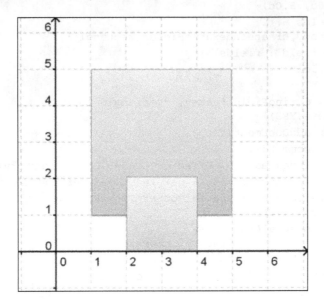

The red square is what we added to the index. The blue square is what we used to search. Since the spatial operation is intersects, we are looking for shapes that intersect with the blue square. This diagram clearly shows that the red square does intersect with the blue square, hence the match.

There's more...

There is more information on spatial search that can be found on Spatial4j's web site: `https://github.com/spatial4j/spatial4j`.

Implementing joins

Join is a relational database concept where data are typically normalized, stored in separate tables for efficiency in storage and maintaining data integrity, and then data are joined together between tables to provide a coherent view of the data. In Lucene, there are no concepts of tables because all the records are supposed to be flattened and stored as documents. Even setting up schema in advance is optional. In a document-based store such as Lucene, joins always seem like an afterthought. However, it doesn't mean that you can't do joins at all in Lucene. There are many techniques to simulate joins such as adding a document type field to identify different types (tables) of records. Then, manually combine data at runtime by issuing multiple search queries retrieving data of different types.

Lucene offers two types of join methods. One is an index-time join where documents are added in blocks; basically, parent record and child record relationships. The other type is query-time join where you combine records based on a specified criteria.

In an index-time join, we need to first identify the parent record and the child records that need to be merged. The child records are then added as subdocuments alongside the parent record in a document block. A document block is a list of document objects with a parent document added at the end of the list. When adding documents to the index, instead of calling `addDocument(Document)` IndexWriter, we will be calling `addDocuments(Iterable<Document>)` to add the document blocks. At search time, we can use `ToParentBlockJoinQuery` to join child queries and roll into a regular query, which is the query against parent documents, as a query clause.

In query-time join, the paradigm is similar to joining tables in a relational database. We will identify a from field and to field as join keys. It'll be a two-pass search where values from the from field are collected from the query, called from the query, and are used to match to the to field in the second pass against the same IndexSearcher.

Getting ready...

Here is the Maven dependency that's needed to start using joins:

```
<dependency>
    <groupId>org.apache.lucene</groupId>
    <artifactId>lucene-join</artifactId>
    <version>VERSION</version>
</dependency>
```

How to do it...

Here is an example of an index-time join:

```
StandardAnalyzer analyzer = new StandardAnalyzer();
Directory directory = new RAMDirectory();
IndexWriterConfig config = new
  IndexWriterConfig(Version.LATEST, analyzer);
IndexWriter indexWriter = new IndexWriter(directory,
  config);

List<Document> documentList = new ArrayList();

Document childDoc1 = new Document();
childDoc1.add(new StringField("name", "Child doc 1",
  Field.Store.YES));
```

```
childDoc1.add(new StringField("type", "child",
  Field.Store.YES));
childDoc1.add(new LongField("points", 10,
  Field.Store.YES));
Document childDoc2 = new Document();
childDoc2.add(new StringField("name", "Child doc 2",
  Field.Store.YES));
childDoc2.add(new StringField("type", "child",
  Field.Store.YES));
childDoc2.add(new LongField("points", 100,
  Field.Store.YES));
Document parentDoc = new Document();
parentDoc.add(new StringField("name", "Parent doc 1",
  Field.Store.YES));
parentDoc.add(new StringField("type", "parent",
  Field.Store.YES));
parentDoc.add(new LongField("points", 1000,
  Field.Store.YES));
documentList.add(childDoc1);
documentList.add(childDoc2);
documentList.add(parentDoc);
indexWriter.addDocuments(documentList);
indexWriter.commit();
IndexReader indexReader =
  DirectoryReader.open(directory);
IndexSearcher indexSearcher = new
  IndexSearcher(indexReader);
Query childQuery = new TermQuery(new Term("type",
  "child"));
Filter parentFilter = new
  FixedBitSetCachingWrapperFilter(new QueryWrapperFilter(new
TermQuery(new Term("type",
  "parent"))));
ToParentBlockJoinQuery toParentBlockJoinQuery = new
  ToParentBlockJoinQuery(childQuery, parentFilter,
    ScoreMode.Max);
ToParentBlockJoinCollector toParentBlockJoinCollector =
  new ToParentBlockJoinCollector(Sort.RELEVANCE, 10,
    true, true);
indexSearcher.search(toParentBlockJoinQuery,
  toParentBlockJoinCollector);
TopGroups topGroups =
  toParentBlockJoinCollector.getTopGroupsWithAllChildDocs
    (toParentBlockJoinQuery, Sort.RELEVANCE, 0, 0, true);
System.out.println("Total group count: " +
  topGroups.totalGroupCount);
```

```
System.out.println("Total hits: " +
  topGroups.totalGroupedHitCount);
Document doc = null;
for (GroupDocs groupDocs : topGroups.groups) {
  doc = indexSearcher.doc((Integer)groupDocs.groupValue);
  System.out.println("parent: " +
  doc.getField("name").stringValue());
  for (ScoreDoc scoreDoc : groupDocs.scoreDocs) {
    doc = indexSearcher.doc(scoreDoc.doc);
    System.out.println(scoreDoc.score + ": " +
      doc.getField("name").stringValue());
  }
}
```

In this example, we added one document block with a parent document and two child documents. The document block is then added by calling `addDocuments`. To query this document block, we use `ToParentBlockJoinQuery` with a child query (query against child records) and a parent filter (filter against parent records). The result is collected using `ToParentBlockJoinQueryCollector`. Note that `parentFilter` is wrapped in `FixedBitSetCachingWrapperFilter`. This is because we need to use a filter that returns `FixedBitSet` in `ToParentBlockJoinQueryCollector`. To retrieve the results, we called `getTopGroupsWithAllChildDocs`, and this method returns `TopGroups` that contains DocId of both parent and child documents. There are two counts in TopGroups: `totalGroupCount`, representing the total count of matching parent documents and `totalGroupedHitCount`, representing the total count of matching child documents.

Here is an example of query-time join:

```
StandardAnalyzer analyzer = new StandardAnalyzer();
Directory directory = new RAMDirectory();
IndexWriterConfig config = new IndexWriterConfig(Version.LATEST,
  analyzer);
IndexWriter indexWriter = new IndexWriter(directory, config);
Document doc = new Document();
doc.add(new StringField("name", "A Book", Field.Store.YES));
doc.add(new StringField("type", "book", Field.Store.YES));
doc.add(new LongField("bookAuthorId", 1, Field.Store.YES));
doc.add(new LongField("bookId", 1, Field.Store.YES));
indexWriter.addDocument(doc);
doc = new Document();
doc.add(new StringField("name", "An Author", Field.Store.YES));
doc.add(new StringField("type", "author", Field.Store.YES));
doc.add(new LongField("authorId", 1, Field.Store.YES));
indexWriter.addDocument(doc);
indexWriter.commit();
```

```
IndexReader indexReader = DirectoryReader.open(directory);
IndexSearcher indexSearcher = new IndexSearcher(indexReader);
String fromField = "bookAuthorId";
boolean multipleValuesPerDocument = false;
String toField = "authorId";
ScoreMode scoreMode = ScoreMode.Max;
Query fromQuery = new TermQuery(new Term("type", "book"));
Query joinQuery = JoinUtil.createJoinQuery(
    fromField,
    multipleValuesPerDocument,
    toField,
    fromQuery,
    indexSearcher,
    scoreMode);
TopDocs topDocs = indexSearcher.search(joinQuery, 10);
System.out.println("Total hits: " + topDocs.totalHits);
for (ScoreDoc scoreDoc : topDocs.scoreDocs) {
    doc = indexReader.document(scoreDoc.doc);
    System.out.println(scoreDoc.score + ": " +
        doc.getField("name").stringValue());
}
```

In this example, we loaded two types of documents into the index. One is a book and another one is an author. The book has a `bookId` and `bookAuthorId` (to link to an author by an `authorId`), and author has an `authorId`. We called a `static` method `JoinUtil.createJoinQuery` to formulate a join query by submitting the `fromField`, `fromQuery`, and `toField`. It's a two-pass search where the first pass is filtered by `fromQuery`, and then the `fromField` values are extracted from the results and are used to match with the `toField` to return the final results. This example will find one result matching the author record.

Performing faceting

Faceting provides a way to drill down data by categories. It allows a user to refine a search by concatenating new categories to narrow down a search to the desired results. A useful feature in faceting is that you can preview the total hits with each category values before selecting it. The faceted search method can be used in conjunction with a text search, so it's okay for users to do a text search in addition to a faceted search at any point. In many search applications where data can be systematically categorized, such as product inventory where you have product categories, types, availability, and so on, faceting offers a convenient way for users to refine their searches. A notable benefit of faceting is that the user will never hit a zero results page because you can only drill down with in the available category values.

Let's look at an example for a fictional online bookstore; we will categorize books by subject and author. In the following figure, note that we have two facets: subject and author. Underneath each facet, you will find facet values along with potential hits next to each value:

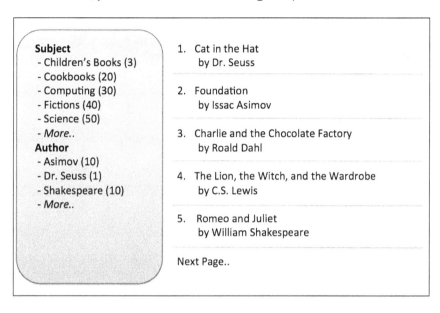

Let's assume a user selects a facet value **Children's Books** under **Subject**. The search will be narrowed down to the following figure:

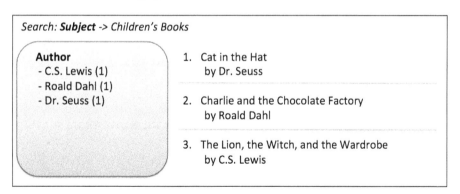

Note that the search result is now narrowed down to three books and the **Author** facet is updated with three remaining values for the three different authors. If you recall from the previous screenshot, the hits for the facet value Children's Books was three. The hits number corresponds to the actual total results after we select Children's Books. A user can further facet search by selecting one of the authors that will narrow down the result to one book. Since there will be no more faceting variations in the result, you will not find any facet values and that'd be the end of the faceting search refinements.

In Lucene, faceting is implemented with two indexes: an index that stores taxonomy (facets) information and a normal index that stores documents. When building facets, we need to define `FacetFields` in category and value pairs and add them to each document. Then, we need to use `FacetsConfig` to build facet values and add to the taxonomy index using a TaxonomyWriter. When executing a faceting search, we can use one of the faceting classes such as FastTaxonomyFacetCount to return facet values and their counts. Because this is a customized search, we will use a dedicated Collector, FacetsCollector, to collect the results.

Getting ready...

Here is the Maven dependency to acquire the library:

```
<dependency>
    <groupId>org.apache.lucene</groupId>
    <artifactId>lucene-facet</artifactId>
    <version>VERSION</version>
</dependency>
```

How to do it...

Let's take a look at some codes:

```
StandardAnalyzer analyzer = new StandardAnalyzer();
Directory indexDirectory = new RAMDirectory();
Directory facetDirectory = new RAMDirectory();
IndexWriterConfig config = new IndexWriterConfig(Version.LATEST,
  analyzer);
IndexWriter indexWriter = new IndexWriter(indexDirectory, config);
DirectoryTaxonomyWriter directoryTaxonomyWriter = new
  DirectoryTaxonomyWriter(facetDirectory);
FacetsConfig facetsConfig = new FacetsConfig();
Document doc = new Document();
doc.add(new StringField("BookId", "B1", Field.Store.YES));
doc.add(new FacetField("Author", "Author 1"));
doc.add(new FacetField("Category", "Cat 1"));
indexWriter.addDocument(facetsConfig.build(directoryTaxonomyWriter
  , doc));
doc = new Document();
doc.add(new StringField("BookId", "B2", Field.Store.YES));
doc.add(new FacetField("Author", "Author 2"));
doc.add(new FacetField("Category", "Cat 1"));
```

```
indexWriter.addDocument(facetsConfig.build(directoryTaxonomyWriter
  , doc));
doc = new Document();
doc.add(new StringField("BookId", "B3", Field.Store.YES));
doc.add(new FacetField("Author", "Author 3"));
doc.add(new FacetField("Category", "Cat 2"));
indexWriter.addDocument(facetsConfig.build(directoryTaxonomyWriter
  , doc));
indexWriter.commit();
directoryTaxonomyWriter.commit();


IndexReader indexReader = DirectoryReader.open(indexDirectory);
IndexSearcher indexSearcher = new IndexSearcher(indexReader);
DirectoryTaxonomyReader directoryTaxonomyReader = new
  DirectoryTaxonomyReader(facetDirectory);
FacetsCollector facetsCollector = new FacetsCollector();
FacetsCollector.search(indexSearcher, new MatchAllDocsQuery(), 10,
  facetsCollector);
Facets facets = new
  FastTaxonomyFacetCounts(directoryTaxonomyReader, facetsConfig,
    facetsCollector);
FacetResult facetResult = facets.getTopChildren(10, "Category");
for (LabelAndValue labelAndValue : facetResult.labelValues) {
  System.out.println(labelAndValue.label + ":" +
    labelAndValue.value);
}
facetResult = facets.getTopChildren(10, "Author");
for (LabelAndValue labelAndValue : facetResult.labelValues) {
  System.out.println(labelAndValue.label + ":" +
    labelAndValue.value);
}


DrillDownQuery drillDownQuery = new DrillDownQuery(facetsConfig);
drillDownQuery.add("Category", "Cat 1");
DrillSideways drillSideways = new DrillSideways(indexSearcher,
  facetsConfig, directoryTaxonomyReader);
DrillSideways.DrillSidewaysResult drillSidewaysResult =
  drillSideways.search(drillDownQuery, 10);


facetResult = drillSidewaysResult.facets.getTopChildren(10,
  "Category");
```

```
for (LabelAndValue labelAndValue : facetResult.labelValues) {
  System.out.println(labelAndValue.label + ":" +
    labelAndValue.value);
}
facetResult = drillSidewaysResult.facets.getTopChildren(10,
  "Author");
for (LabelAndValue labelAndValue : facetResult.labelValues) {
  System.out.println(labelAndValue.label + ":" +
    labelAndValue.value);
}
```

How it works...

We set up two facets, **author** and **category**, in this demonstration. Note that we have two Directories: `indexDirectory` and `facetDirectory`. For the `facetDirectory`, we set up `DirectoryTaxonomyWriter` to index facets. We added three documents, all with two FacetFields. Note how we build facets with `FacetsConfig.build` to write to the `TaxonomyWriter`.

In data retrieval, we instantiated DirectoryTaxonomyReader and FacetsCollector to retrieve facet information. We called `FacetsCollector.search` to perform faceting search and `FastTaxonomyFacetCounts` to render the results into facet values. We used `FastTaxonomyFacetCounts` to retrieve hits per facet value, which is similar to the bookstore application illustrated in this section. The first set of output would produce the following:

```
Cat 1:2
Cat 2:1
Author 1:1
Author 2:1
Author 3:1
```

These are facet values and their hit counts. The `Cat 1` has 2 because we have two records, B1 and B2, where their Category value is `Cat 1`.

In the second test, we used `DrillDownQuery` and `DrillSideways` to select a facet value to drill down and return the available facet values. We picked `Cat 1` in our `DrillDownQuery` and we called `DrillSideways.search` to return the remaining facet values, which is after selecting `Cat 1`. The resulting output would produce the following:

```
Cat 1:2
Cat 2:1
Author 1:1
Author 2:1
```

We still see the category facet, although we selected `Cat 1` because the values are shown based on an assumption that when you select a different category value, it would replace the existing one that's been selected. This is more of a usability suggestion. In some implementations, categories where their values are selected are actually filtered out. The facet that's of interest in this scenario is Author. Notice we only see `Author 1` and `Author 2`. That's because both of these authors contain `Cat 1`, while `Author 3` has `Cat 2`. We selected `Cat 1` in our facet search, hence the omission.

Implementing grouping

The Grouping feature in Lucene offers a way to group results together by a group field. Say you may want to list books by category so it'd be convenient to display results when the resulting documents are already grouped by the group field. Another example is a web search engine where results may be grouped by sites, so a site with excessive numbers of matching pages does not overwhelm the top result page. The search engine can show the top matching page from each site so there is more variety of quality matches.

Lucene has two implementations for grouping a single-pass search and a two-pass search. A single-pass search requires document grouping at index time and a two-pass search requires two searches to provide both group-level and document-level results.

To set up a single-pass search, we will add a document in document blocks by calling `IndexWriter.addDocuments`. We also need to add an end of the document marker, as Field, to the last document in each document block to aid a group search. The end of the document marker is then passed into BlockGroupingCollector as a Filter so it can retrieve group-level data. One caveat of this method is that the GroupDocs.groupValue field is null so, to return a group-level value, we will have to pull from one of the documents within a group or FieldCache.

A two-pass search is more flexible as it does not require any augmentation at index-time. Instead of using BlockGroupingCollector, we can use GroupingSearch, which implements a two-pass search internally instead. In a two-pass search, GroupDocs.groupValue contains the group value in BytesRef.

Getting ready...

Here is the Maven dependency to acquire the Grouping library:

```
<dependency>
    <groupId>org.apache.lucene</groupId>
    <artifactId>lucene-grouping</artifactId>
    <version>VERSION</version>
</dependency>
```

How to do it...

Let's first take a look at a single-pass search using BlockGroupingCollector:

```
StandardAnalyzer analyzer = new StandardAnalyzer();
Directory directory = new RAMDirectory();
IndexWriterConfig config = new IndexWriterConfig(Version.LATEST,
  analyzer);
IndexWriter indexWriter = new IndexWriter(directory, config);

FieldType groupEndFieldType = new FieldType();
groupEndFieldType.setStored(false);
groupEndFieldType.setTokenized(false);
groupEndFieldType.setIndexed(true);
groupEndFieldType.setIndexOptions(FieldInfo.IndexOptions.DOCS_ONLY
  );
groupEndFieldType.setOmitNorms(true);
Field groupEndField = new Field("groupEnd", "x",
  groupEndFieldType);

List<Document> documentList = new ArrayList();
Document doc = new Document();
doc.add(new StringField("BookId", "B1", Field.Store.YES));
doc.add(new StringField("Category", "Cat 1", Field.Store.YES));
documentList.add(doc);
doc = new Document();
doc.add(new StringField("BookId", "B2", Field.Store.YES));
doc.add(new StringField("Category", "Cat 1", Field.Store.YES));
documentList.add(doc);
doc.add(groupEndField);
indexWriter.addDocuments(documentList);

documentList = new ArrayList();
doc = new Document();
doc.add(new StringField("BookId", "B3", Field.Store.YES));
doc.add(new StringField("Category", "Cat 2", Field.Store.YES));
documentList.add(doc);
doc.add(groupEndField);
indexWriter.addDocuments(documentList);

indexWriter.commit();
```

```
Filter groupEndDocs = new CachingWrapperFilter(new
  QueryWrapperFilter(new TermQuery(new Term("groupEnd", "x")))));

IndexReader indexReader = DirectoryReader.open(directory);
IndexSearcher indexSearcher = new IndexSearcher(indexReader);

BlockGroupingCollector blockGroupingCollector = new
  BlockGroupingCollector(Sort.RELEVANCE, 10, true, groupEndDocs);
indexSearcher.search(new MatchAllDocsQuery(), null,
  blockGroupingCollector);

TopGroups topGroups = blockGroupingCollector.getTopGroups(Sort.
RELEVANCE, 0, 0, 10,
  true);

System.out.println("Total group count: " +
  topGroups.totalGroupCount);
System.out.println("Total group hit count: " +
  topGroups.totalGroupedHitCount);

for (GroupDocs groupDocs : topGroups.groups) {
    System.out.println("Group: " + groupDocs.groupValue);
    for (ScoreDoc scoreDoc : groupDocs.scoreDocs) {
        doc = indexSearcher.doc(scoreDoc.doc);
        System.out.println("Category: " +
  doc.getField("Category").stringValue() + ", BookId: " +
    doc.getField("BookId").stringValue());
    }
}
```

We first set up a field called `groupEndField` as a marker for the end of the group in a document block. This Field is attached to the last document as we create the document blocks. The documents are grouped by the `Cat 1` and `Cat 2` categories. Then, we created a `groupEndDocs` filter to aid `BlockGroupingCollector` in identifying groups. IndexSearcher is used to execute a search as usual, but we would use BlockGroupingCollector to collect the results. Then, we called `getTopGroups` to return TopGroups (analogous to TopDocs, but for groups) where we retrieve group-level results such as group count, group hit count, and documents within each group.

Here is an example of a two-pass search:

```
StandardAnalyzer analyzer = new StandardAnalyzer();
Directory directory = new RAMDirectory();
IndexWriterConfig config = new IndexWriterConfig(Version.LATEST,
  analyzer);
```

```
IndexWriter indexWriter = new IndexWriter(directory, config);
Document doc = new Document();
doc.add(new StringField("BookId", "B1", Field.Store.YES));
doc.add(new StringField("Category", "Cat 1", Field.Store.YES));
indexWriter.addDocument(doc);
doc = new Document();
doc.add(new StringField("BookId", "B2", Field.Store.YES));
doc.add(new StringField("Category", "Cat 1", Field.Store.YES));
indexWriter.addDocument(doc);
doc = new Document();
doc.add(new StringField("BookId", "B3", Field.Store.YES));
doc.add(new StringField("Category", "Cat 2", Field.Store.YES));
indexWriter.addDocument(doc);
indexWriter.commit();
GroupingSearch groupingSearch = new GroupingSearch("Category");
groupingSearch.setAllGroups(true);
groupingSearch.setGroupDocsLimit(10);
IndexReader indexReader = DirectoryReader.open(directory);
IndexSearcher indexSearcher = new IndexSearcher(indexReader);
TopGroups topGroups = groupingSearch.search(indexSearcher, new
  MatchAllDocsQuery(), 0, 10);
System.out.println("Total group count: " +
  topGroups.totalGroupCount);
System.out.println("Total group hit count: " +
  topGroups.totalGroupedHitCount);
for (GroupDocs groupDocs : topGroups.groups) {
  System.out.println("Group: " +
    ((BytesRef)groupDocs.groupValue).utf8ToString());
  for (ScoreDoc scoreDoc : groupDocs.scoreDocs) {
  doc = indexSearcher.doc(scoreDoc.doc);
  System.out.println("Category: " +
    doc.getField("Category").stringValue() + ", BookId: " +
      doc.getField("BookId").stringValue());
  }
}
```

In this example, we added documents to the index as normal (no document blocks). Then, we used a class called `GroupingSearch` to execute a group search. This class implements a two-pass search internally so we only have to call search once to return the search results. To get the total group count, we enabled the all groups flag by calling `groupingSearch.setAllGroups(true)`. Then, we executed the search and returned TopGroups, which we can iterate through to return grouped documents. Note that in this example, we retrieved groupValue as BytesRef so we could display the group value in our iteration.

Employing autosuggest

Lucene's suggest module offers a number of implementations that can be used to support a real-time autosuggest feature when a user types into a search box. You will find many tools in the suggest module that helps facilitate the data ingestion process to the autosuggest index. In our demonstrations, we will be using LuceneDictionary to ingest data as it provides the convenience of extracting tokens from a field in an existing index.

We will go over four suggester implementations in this section:

▶ **AnalyzingSuggester**: This suggester analyzes input text and provides suggestions based on prefixed matches.

▶ **AnalyzingInfixSuggester**: This suggester builds on top of AnalyzingSuggester and provides suggestions based on the prefix matches in any tokens in the indexed text.

▶ **FreeTextSuggester**: This suggester is an n-gram implementation that produces suggestions based on matches to an N-gram index. N-gram is a contiguous sequence of n items from a given text sequence. "n" represents the number of items in the indexing sequence. In this implementation, the default configuration uses a bigram model (sequence of 2). It can be changed to use trigram (3) if desired.

▶ **FuzzySuggester**: This suggester builds on top of AnalyzingSuggester performing a fuzzy search that will match terms up to 2 edits.

These suggesters all have their own strengths and weaknesses; a robust application may use one or more of these suggesters to provide a good user experience. For example, one may want to use AnalyzingSuggester first to find matches as user types and, when no more suggestions are found, we may want to switch to FreeTextSuggester or FuzzySuggester to find more potential matches. Maximizing potential matches usually helps to improve the user experience.

Getting ready...

Here is the Maven dependency to acquire the suggest module;

```
<dependency>
    <groupId>org.apache.lucene</groupId>
    <artifactId>lucene-suggest</artifactId>
    <version>${lucene.version}</version>
</dependency>
```

We will set up our tests with the following code to initialize the index:

```
StandardAnalyzer analyzer = new StandardAnalyzer();
Directory directory = new RAMDirectory();
IndexWriterConfig config = new IndexWriterConfig(Version.LATEST,
    analyzer);
IndexWriter indexWriter = new IndexWriter(directory, config);
Document doc = new Document();
doc.add(new StringField("content", "Humpty Dumpty sat on a wall",
    Field.Store.YES));
indexWriter.addDocument(doc);
doc = new Document();
doc.add(new StringField("content", "Humpty Dumpty had a great
    fall", Field.Store.YES));
indexWriter.addDocument(doc);
doc = new Document();
doc.add(new StringField("content", "All the king's horses and all
    the king's men", Field.Store.YES));
indexWriter.addDocument(doc);
doc = new Document();
doc.add(new StringField("content", "Couldn't put Humpty together
    again", Field.Store.YES));
indexWriter.addDocument(doc);
indexWriter.commit();
indexWriter.close();
IndexReader indexReader = DirectoryReader.open(directory);
Dictionary dictionary = new LuceneDictionary(indexReader,
    "content");
```

Here, we set up the index as usual with a number of documents and we open an IndexReader and initialize a dictionary object to be passed on to the suggesters to build their internal index.

How to do it...

Here is an example of AnalyzingSuggester:

```
AnalyzingSuggester analyzingSuggester = new AnalyzingSuggester(new
    StandardAnalyzer());
analyzingSuggester.build(dictionary);

List<Lookup.LookupResult> lookupResultList =
    analyzingSuggester.lookup("humpty dum", false, 10);

for (Lookup.LookupResult lookupResult : lookupResultList) {
    System.out.println(lookupResult.key + ": " +
        lookupResult.value);
}
```

This is a simple demonstration of how easy it is to initialize an AnalyzingSuggester with an Analyzer and a Dictionary. The same Analyzer should be used between indexing search and suggester as this will help ensure suggestion accuracy. Once the suggester is loaded with data, we can perform a lookup to find the potential matches. In this case, it should return the following result for humpty dum:

```
Humpty Dumpty had a great fall: 1
Humpty Dumpty sat on a wall: 1
```

Since this is a prefix match, the terms humpty dum matches the prefixes for these two field values. Note that the value in LookupResult is the weight of the match.

Let's look at an example of AnalyzingInfixSuggester:

```
AnalyzingInfixSuggester analyzingInfixSuggester = new
  AnalyzingInfixSuggester(Version.LATEST, directory, analyzer);
analyzingInfixSuggester.build(dictionary);

List<Lookup.LookupResult> lookupResultList =
  analyzingInfixSuggester.lookup("put h", false, 10);

for (Lookup.LookupResult lookupResult : lookupResultList) {
  System.out.println(lookupResult.key + ": " +
    lookupResult.value);
}
```

The code structure is similar to the exception of the constructor where, this time, we need to pass in a version, directory, and an analyser. The test search string we use in this case is put h. This demonstrates this suggester's ability to match tokens anywhere within a string. It should output the following:

```
Couldn't put Humpty together again: 1
```

Next, we will look at FreeTextSuggester:

```
FreeTextSuggester freeTextSuggester = new FreeTextSuggester(analyzer,
analyzer, 3);
freeTextSuggester.build(dictionary);

List<Lookup.LookupResult> lookupResultList = freeTextSuggester.
lookup("h", false, 10);

for (Lookup.LookupResult lookupResult : lookupResultList) {
    System.out.println(lookupResult.key + ": " + lookupResult.value);
}
```

The `FreeTextSuggester` constructor requires an analyzer for both index and query. The last number indicates the N in n-gram. In our test, we change from the default of bigram to trigram (3). Then, we look up suggestion matching `h`, and here is the output with terms matching `h`:

```
humpty: 1383505805528216320
had: 461168601842738816
horses: 461168601842738816
```

Lastly, we will look at FuzzySuggester:

```
FuzzySuggester fuzzySuggester = new FuzzySuggester(new
    StandardAnalyzer());
fuzzySuggester.build(dictionary);
List<Lookup.LookupResult> lookupResultList =
    fuzzySuggester.lookup("hampty", false, 10);
for (Lookup.LookupResult lookupResult : lookupResultList) {
    System.out.println(lookupResult.key + ": " +
        lookupResult.value);
}
```

This test demonstrates fuzzy term matching. The search term hampty is misspelled on purpose. This code will produce the following output:

```
Humpty Dumpty had a great fall: 1
Humpty Dumpty sat on a wall: 1
```

Implementing highlighting

Highlighting offers the ability to highlight search terms in results, in order to show where matches occur. It helps to improve the user experience by allowing a user to see how matching documents are found. This is especially useful when displaying a text result that contains several lines of text.

The highlighting feature starts with the highlighter class. It can be configured with a formatter and an encoder to render the results. Then, we retrieve a TokenStream from the matching Field and pass it on to the Highlighter to render highlighting results.

Getting ready...

Here is the Maven dependency:

```
<dependency>
    <groupId>org.apache.lucene</groupId>
    <artifactId>lucene-highlighter</artifactId>
    <version>${lucene.version}</version>
</dependency>
```

How to do it...

Let's take a look at a sample implementation:

```
StandardAnalyzer analyzer = new StandardAnalyzer();
Directory directory = new RAMDirectory();
IndexWriterConfig config = new IndexWriterConfig(Version.LATEST,
  analyzer);
IndexWriter indexWriter = new IndexWriter(directory, config);
Document doc = new Document();
doc.add(new TextField("content", "Humpty Dumpty sat on a wall",
  Field.Store.YES));
indexWriter.addDocument(doc);
doc = new Document();
doc.add(new TextField("content", "Humpty Dumpty had a great fall",
  Field.Store.YES));
indexWriter.addDocument(doc);
doc = new Document();
doc.add(new TextField("content", "All the king's horses and all
  the king's men", Field.Store.YES));
indexWriter.addDocument(doc);
doc = new Document();
doc.add(new TextField("content", "Couldn't put Humpty together
  again", Field.Store.YES));
indexWriter.addDocument(doc);
indexWriter.commit();
indexWriter.close();
IndexReader indexReader = DirectoryReader.open(directory);
IndexSearcher indexSearcher = new IndexSearcher(indexReader);
Query query = new TermQuery(new Term("content", "humpty"));
TopDocs topDocs = indexSearcher.search(query, 10);
SimpleHTMLFormatter simpleHTMLFormatter = new
  SimpleHTMLFormatter("<strong>", "</strong>");
SimpleHTMLEncoder simpleHTMLEncoder = new SimpleHTMLEncoder();
Highlighter highlighter = new Highlighter(simpleHTMLFormatter,
  simpleHTMLEncoder, new QueryScorer(query));
for (ScoreDoc scoreDoc : topDocs.scoreDocs) {
  doc = indexSearcher.doc(scoreDoc.doc);
  String text = doc.get("content");
  TokenStream tokenStream =
    TokenSources.getAnyTokenStream(indexReader, scoreDoc.doc,
      "content", analyzer);
```

```
TextFragment[] textFragments =
  highlighter.getBestTextFragments(tokenStream, text, false,
    10);
for (TextFragment textFragment : textFragments) {
  if (textFragment != null && textFragment.getScore() > 0) {
    System.out.println(textFragment.toString());
  }
}
}
```

How it works...

We have the usual setup for this test. In Highlighter initialization, we used both SimpleHTMLFormatter and SimpleHTMLEncoder to help render the results. The SimpleHTMLFormatter inserts a pre-tag and post-tag to wrap around search terms. In our case, we customized it to wrap each search term with the <strong> tag. The SimpleHTMLEncoder encodes a special character in HTML form. We also passed in a QueryScorer to help identify search terms in Query that generates hits.

In our results rendering, we iterated TopDocs and used IndexSearcher to return a document so we can retrieve a field value. To help improve performance, you may want to use FieldCache to pull a value from the memory. Then, we leveraged TokenSources to return a TokenStream from the IndexReader on the "content" Field (one that we searched against). TokenStream was passed into Highlighter to generate the highlighted output. The returning TextFragment contains the fragment with highlighted terms and a score. A score is only assigned on TextFragment when a matching search term is found. A score is assigned by QueryScorer.

Index

A

abstract class
  acceptsDocsOutOfOrder() 82
  collect(int) 82
  setNextReader(AtomicReaderContext) 82
  setScorer(Scorer) 82
acquire 90
action types
  create 162
  delete 162
  index 162
  update 162
advanced filtering
  performing 102-108
analysis process
  defining 24
analyzer
  creating 12, 13
analyzers, Lucene
  SimpleAnalyzer 26
  SnowballAnalyzer 26
  StandardAnalyzer 26
  StopAnalyzer 26
  WhitespaceAnalyzer 26
arguments, filter 110
autogenerated phrase query 115
autosuggest implementations
  AnalyzingInfixSuggester 189
  AnalyzingSuggester 189
  FreeTextSuggester 189
  FuzzySuggester 189
autosuggest module
  employing 189-192

B

Backus Normal Form (BNF) 18
BBoxStrategy 172
BM25 model
  about 139
  implementing 140-142
Boolean model (BM) 130
BooleanQuery 118, 119
boosting
  about 58
  index time boost 58
  query time boost 58
built-in filters, Lucene
  CachingWrapperFilter 103
  defining 102
  FieldCacheRangeFilter 102
  FieldCacheTermsFilter 103
  FieldValueFilter 103
  NumericRangeFilter 102
  PrefixFilter 103
  QueryWrapperFilter 103
  TermRangeFilter 102
built-in spatial strategies
  BBoxStrategy 172
  PointVectorStrategy 172
  PrefixTreeStrategy 173, 174
  SerializedDVStrategy 174
bulk indexing
  performing 162-164

K

Kibana 152
KinoSearch
  URL 7

L

language model
  about 140
  implementing 143-145
latency
  about 97-99
  benefits 98
lengthNorm 131
Logstash 152
lowercase expanded term 117
Lucene
  about 2, 3, 88, 102
  features 5
  implementations 6
  installing 7
  official page 7
  three stage process flow 3
  URL 27
  working 3
Lucene4c
  URL 6
LuceneKit
  URL 6
Lucene.Net
  URL 6
Lucene QueryParser
  queries, creating with 18
Lupy
  URL 6

M

Maven repository
  URL 10
Montezuma
  URL 7
MultiPhraseQuery
  defining 119
MUTIS
  URL 7

N

new index
  creating 155, 156
NLucene
  URL 7
node 167
norms
  calculating 58
NRT
  about 88, 99
  benefits 99
  DirectoryReader used, for opening
      index in 88-90
numeric field
  creating 49, 50
NumericRangeQuery
  defining 121

O

Object Oriented Programming (OOP) 4
Okapi BM25 139
OpenMode options
  APPEND 46
  CREATE 46
  CREATE_OR_APPEND 46
ordered tree data structure 49

P

pagination 78-80
PerFieldAnalyzerWrapper
  example 34
  using 34-36
performance
  improving 98
PhraseQuery
  defining 119
phrase slop 117
Plucene
  URL 7
plugins, Elasticsearch
  URL 155
PointVectorStrategy 172
PositionIncrementAttribute
  using 32-34

Thank you for buying
Lucene 4 Cookbook

About Packt Publishing

Packt, pronounced 'packed', published its first book, *Mastering phpMyAdmin for Effective MySQL Management*, in April 2004, and subsequently continued to specialize in publishing highly focused books on specific technologies and solutions.

Our books and publications share the experiences of your fellow IT professionals in adapting and customizing today's systems, applications, and frameworks. Our solution-based books give you the knowledge and power to customize the software and technologies you're using to get the job done. Packt books are more specific and less general than the IT books you have seen in the past. Our unique business model allows us to bring you more focused information, giving you more of what you need to know, and less of what you don't.

Packt is a modern yet unique publishing company that focuses on producing quality, cutting-edge books for communities of developers, administrators, and newbies alike. For more information, please visit our website at www.packtpub.com.

About Packt Open Source

In 2010, Packt launched two new brands, Packt Open Source and Packt Enterprise, in order to continue its focus on specialization. This book is part of the Packt open source brand, home to books published on software built around open source licenses, and offering information to anybody from advanced developers to budding web designers. The Open Source brand also runs Packt's open source Royalty Scheme, by which Packt gives a royalty to each open source project about whose software a book is sold.

Writing for Packt

We welcome all inquiries from people who are interested in authoring. Book proposals should be sent to author@packtpub.com. If your book idea is still at an early stage and you would like to discuss it first before writing a formal book proposal, then please contact us; one of our commissioning editors will get in touch with you.

We're not just looking for published authors; if you have strong technical skills but no writing experience, our experienced editors can help you develop a writing career, or simply get some additional reward for your expertise.

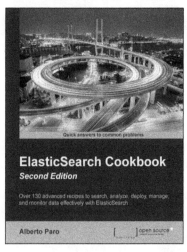

Mastering Elasticsearch
Second Edition

ISBN: 978-1-78355-379-2   Paperback: 434 pages

Further your knowledge of the Elasticsearch server by learning more about its internals, querying, and data handling

1. Understand Apache Lucene and Elasticsearch's design and architecture.

2. Design your index, configure it, and distribute it, not only with assumptions, but with the underlying knowledge of how it works.

3. Improve your user search experience with Elasticsearch functionality and learn how to develop your own Elasticsearch plugins.

Scaling Apache Solr

ISBN: 978-1-78398-174-8   Paperback: 298 pages

Optimize your searches using high-performance enterprise search repositories with Apache Solr

1. Get an introduction to the basics of Apache Solr in a step-by-step manner with lots of examples.

2. Develop and understand the workings of enterprise search solution using various techniques and real-life use cases.

3. Gain a practical insight into the advanced ways of optimizing and making an enterprise search solution cloud ready.

Please check **www.PacktPub.com** for information on our titles